BAD BOYFRIENDS

Using Attachment Theory to
Avoid Mr. (or Ms.) Wrong and
Make You a Better Partner

Jeb Kinnison

BAD BOYFRIENDS

Using Attachment Theory to
Avoid Mr. (or Ms.) Wrong and
Make You a Better Partner

Jeb Kinnison

Table of Contents

Author's Note

Human loneliness is one of the hidden problems of our technologically advanced and mobile age—as our lives get more complicated and our neighborhood of friends has expanded to include social networks, the loss of community feeling to busyness and isolated lives is acutely felt. In this detached world, a good partner, companion, or spouse is more important than ever.

Most people are unaware of modern Attachment Theory, developed starting in the 1940s by psychoanalyst John Bowlby observing the homeless and orphaned children of World War II, further developed in children by developmental psychologist Mary Ainsworth in the 1970s, and extended to adults by Cindy Hazan and Phillip Shaver in the late 1980s. While there have been some efforts to explain the theory to the lay audience who could surely apply it usefully in their lives, it remains obscure.

This book was written to explain attachment theory (and its application to relationships) to those searching for loyal and trustworthy companions in life. Far too many friends and neighbors have floundered with relationship issues that sap them of energy and make them unhappy. Not every such problem can be solved, but knowing what the landscape of attachment looks like can guide one to a better way of communicating, and a better way of living.

Foreward

This book is intended to be a practical guide to using the modern science of attachment and relationships to guide the questioning toward a more fulfilling life.

If you were brought up in the Western world, you've been trained on fairy tales of love and relationships that are misleading at best, and at worst have you making mistake after mistake in starting relationships with the wrong kinds of people who will waste your time and keep you from finding a loyal partner. Science has the answer! Or at least a guide to save you the time and effort of discovering for yourself how many wrong types of romantic partners there are.

Reading this book will help you recognize the signs of some of the syndromes that prevent people from being good partners. We'll go through those syndromes and point out some of the signs. Those little red flags you sometimes notice when you are getting to know someone? Often they speak loud and clear once you understand the types, and you can decide immediately to run away or approach with caution those who show them.

If you're young and just starting to look for a partner, good news —the world is swarming with well-adjusted, charming matches for you, if you know how to recognize them. The bad news: you are inexperienced and you may not recognize the right type of person when you date them. Many people expect to experience an immediate sense of excitement, an overwhelming rush of attraction, and to fall in love rapidly and equally with someone who feels the same. *This rarely happens, and when it does it usually ends badly!* And expecting it will cause you to let go of people who are steady, loving, and attentive, if you had given them a chance. So once you've identified someone who makes you laugh, answers your messages, and is there for you when you want them, don't make the mistake of tossing them aside for the merely good-looking, sexy, or intriguing stranger. Many friends I have known coupled up with the wrong person and took up to twenty years to realize it before finally giving up and divorcing, because they didn't know their dysfunctional relationship didn't have to be that way, and so they stuck with it far longer than they should have, hoping it would get better.

If you're older, bad news: while you were spending time and effort on relationships you were hoping would turn out better, or even happily nestled in a good relationship or two, most of the secure, reliable, sane people in your age group got paired off. They're married or happily enfamilied, and most of the people your age in the dating pool are tragically unable to form a good long-term relationship. You should always ask yourself, "why is this one still available?"—there may be a good answer (recently widowed or left a long-term relationship), or it may be that this person has just been extraordinarily unlucky in having over twenty short relationships in twenty years (to cite one case!) But it's far more likely you have met someone with a problematic attachment style. As you age past 40, the percentage of the dating pool that is able to form a secure, stable relationship drops to less than 20%[1]; and since it can take months of dating to understand why Mr. or Ms. SeemsNice is really the future ex-partner from Hell, being able to recognize the difficult types will help you recognize them faster and move on to the next.

This book outlines the basics (which might be all you need), and points you toward more resources if you want to understand more about your problem partner. If you're wondering if the guy or girl you've been hanging out with might not be quite right, this is the place to match those little red flags you've noticed with known bad types. And by getting out fast, you can avoid emotional damage and wasted time, and get going on finding someone who's really right for you. Study all of the bad types and you'll detect them before even getting involved. Or you could be one of the people who recognizes their own problems in one of these types. There are study materials and plans of action for you, too. If you've had lots of relationships and they all seem to go wrong, the common factor is you! Your task is to make yourself into a better partner - a goal that even the most evolved of us can always work toward.

I promised you Science! And here's some that is very good to know: *Attachment Theory*. Psychologists have noticed that children whose caregivers (generally, mothers) were either unresponsive to their needs or overly concerned by their needs tended to have children with problems relating to others in a secure way.

- If the child's needs had been ignored or only grudgingly attended to, the child would be *avoidant*—meaning the child would stop seeking comfort, or ignore the caregiver.
- Children who are given a mix of comfort when needed and inattention or unwanted attention inconsistently often end up *anxious-preoccupied*—the child is afraid and needs constant reassurance to feel safe, often clinging to the caregiver and being too afraid to explore out of sight.
- A *secure* child, on the other hand, was used to having

their cries met with comfort and assistance, but only when needed, and learned the language of love— messages of "I'm here if you need me," and "You're safe." Secure children eventually feel safe enough to explore and leave the caregiver's side without fear, since they know their cries will be heard and responded to even from a distance.

In the late 80s, this understanding of children's attachment types was extended to adults. Early upbringing tends to set up the emotional mechanisms for handling all significant relationships, with an adult's style of handling partner and even friendship relationships heavily influenced by the patterns learned in early childhood. And adults with secure patterns have more satisfying, lasting, and successful relationships than adults with other patterns. Later chapters describe each of the adult attachment types and how you can recognize them; your match with another's type is critical to making a relationship work.

And aside from attachment types that are wrong for you, there are the truly hazardous   people with abnormal psychologies who are not crazy enough to be in jail or an institution, but who can be charming and lead apparently successful lives while still being dangerous to your mental health and wellbeing should you be so unlucky as to find yourself in a relationship with one. Remember that in normal life, we use politeness and social manners to avoid knowing too much about the hundreds of people we have to deal with; those with *psychopathologies* can pass for normal for long periods of time in common everyday interactions, and if careful can avoid detection by most people. So your psychopathic neighbor gets along reasonably well at school or church or business, while quietly hurting small animals, and no one's the wiser — until you date him or her. Under this category of Really Bad Potential Partners we have *psychopaths, sadists,* those with *histrionic personality disorder,* and the extremely common *abusive narcissist.* Each of these gets their own chapter.

And if it turns out YOU are the problem—you recognize yourself in one of the case studies, you show the signs and mental habits of being a bad partner and you've failed in multiple relationships because something always seems to go wrong—there's hope for you. Your task is to overcome these bad mental habits and make yourself into the kind of person whose feelings and loyalties can be relied on, who can be a good partner to someone else. And then you will find someone who deserves you.

This book is designed to give you the information you need to find your best partner. The field of attachment studies, and the science of human emotion, is growing rapidly and if you'd like to know more and are interested in deeper readings, check out the references and bibliography. *A General Theory of Love*, by Thomas Lewis, M.D., *et. al.,* is a great introduction.

In general, male and female pronouns will be used interchangeably, except when a syndrome is most commonly demonstrated in one sex—dismissives, for example, are more likely males, while the stereotypical histrionic personality is female. There are always exceptions to these stereotypes. There is also nothing different in attachment terms about gay or lesbian relationships. Most likely readers of this book are female —as is generally true of self-help books, but especially those on relationship-oriented topics. But men can also be puzzled and need knowledge when their partners have a troublesome attachment style, so welcome, men.

Any examples in this book, while drawn from real life, are

fictional—the names, chronologies, and details have been changed.

PART ONE

EMOTIONAL COMMUNICATION

Before we start talking about attachment types in detail, let's cover some background in neuroscience and communication and how people regulate their degree of intimacy with others. Exciting new research into brain structure, development, and function is recent years has complicated the simple model of the *triune brain* that I present here, but it is still a useful model for how instinct, emotion, and rational thought interact.

And while I will focus on the effect of early caregiving on the attachment type of adults, there is almost certainly some genetic component—some people are born with a tendency to security despite caregiving lapses, while others may have reasonably good parenting yet still end up insecure in adulthood. But it is clear that early caregiving has a critically important effect on adult security and attachment type.

CHAPTER ONE

THE TRIUNE BRAIN

Human brains have three main parts: first to evolve was the core *reptilian brain*, which handles basic functioning of the body and primitive reflexes; all vertebrate animals have this. Next came the *limbic system,* developed to a greater extent in mammals, which handles emotional and basic social functioning. Layered on top of that is the *neocortex* ("new brain"), which was last to evolve in mammals but is massively more developed in the human family tree; this huge new brain annex handles the verbal and intellectual processing that sets us apart from other mammals.[2]

Recent research complicates this picture. The human brain (and all brains) are complex systems resulting from the differentiation of neural stem cells, programmed with simple rules to operate in response to their chemical and electrical environment. These rules are set forth in the genes, but during the massive proliferation of new neurons both before birth and after, neurons form patterns and layers, structures and pathways, far more complex than we can truly understand as yet, and then are further winnowed and modified by early training. Neuroscientists attempt to understand the function of each part, but while we may be correct in saying the brainstem ("reptilian brain") is primarily coordinating the autonomic nervous system that keeps all animal bodies functioning, it is more complexly connected than that, and similarly the cortex and cerebellum are connected and evolved to function together, so it is an oversimplification to say the limbic system is "located" in the cerebellum. The functional distinctions are useful in understanding how our senses, actions, and plans are coordinated, but not rigidly reflected in the brain's structure.[3]

Our consciousness and verbalism are recent additions to our species. It is easy to forget that all of our thoughts and the streams of words and symbols that run through our heads when we are "thinking" are easily overruled by the more primitive sublayers, which were designed to keep us alive and compel nonverbal, unthought reactions in the case of threat. Our limbic system, in particular, keeps track of the world around us and reacts to what is sensed to produce emotions to attract, repel, attack, or embrace.

Attachment is a limbic phenomenon; love is deeper than words, and sometimes beyond our ability to verbalize. The dance of signals between mother and child in the child's first years develops the child's emotional system and its emotional response to other human beings, and while children can learn from all of the caregivers in their lives, the first is the most important. Children who are not touched and responded to in early life often sicken and die. And children who are given the wrong kinds of signals will spend a lifetime being lonely or having trouble with their partners as a result.

Chapter Two

People Who Need People

Our culture is full of models and stories about love and relationships. First there's the "fairy tale" of two lovers finding their uniquely perfect partner, falling madly and mutually "in love" (before they can possibly really know each other), and living happily ever after in a cottage with a white picket fence. While this does happen, it's not common, and real tales of love and long-term partnership are rarely so simple and sweet. Then there's the recent hubbub over "codependence"—an idea which began in addiction studies, where an alcoholic, drug addict, or other self-destructive person is enabled by a partner who works to prevent the addict from either getting better or reaching the point of despair sufficient to convince the addict to start anew. Is dependence on another a bad thing, or unhealthy as sometimes implied? No, of course not —we are all dependent as children, and depend on each other more or less our entire lives to accomplish things and feel happy. In a theme we'll return to over and over, being dependent on a reliable person when you need it is good. Being unable to function without the support of others when you need to is bad. As noted later, the most secure children are raised by mothers who seem to sense it almost before their child needs help and assist immediately and just enough, while not hovering or invading the child's independence when they are exploring the world just fine alone. We see that the same "just when needed, just the right amount" principle of dependence acts between the best partners, and best friends. The best partner is responsive to your signals, and you as a good partner signal only when you really need help. Most of the trouble in relationships is about bad signaling and poor responses.

Chapter Three

Touch and Response

The basics of affect regulation (the patterns of signals between people which regulate the feelings they have for each other) were set forth by Mikulincer, Shaver, and Pereg.[4] It is both obvious and profound: it seems so simple as to not be worth describing, and yet underlying almost all our emotional signals to each other is one of these basic templates. Recognize these and you will understand why intentionally holding back on a response is alienating, why constant messages asking for reassurance can drive even the most patient partner away, and how we unconsciously "manage" our relationships by drawing others closer or pushing them away using these patterns. The simplest view is that a partner who is anxious sends a message to the other asking "Are you there?", and either gets a response "I am here for you" and is thus reassured, or gets no response or a negative response, and thus grows more anxious.

There are three basic strategies discussed in this section:[5]
- Security-based strategy
- Hyperactivation, or Anxiety-Attachment strategy
- Attachment-avoidance strategy

The flowchart for the **security-based** strategy:

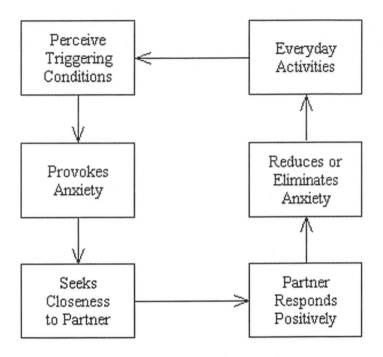

One partner's anxiety is triggered by external problems or simply a lack of recent reassurance. He or she signals (by moving closer, or asking for reassurance, or sending a message) the other partner, who responds with a message of reassurance (by snuggling closer, or saying something supportive, or sending a positive message back). Reassured, life goes on for both of them and anxiety-producing threats are dealt with.

The flowchart for **hyperactivation**, or the anxiety-attachment strategy:

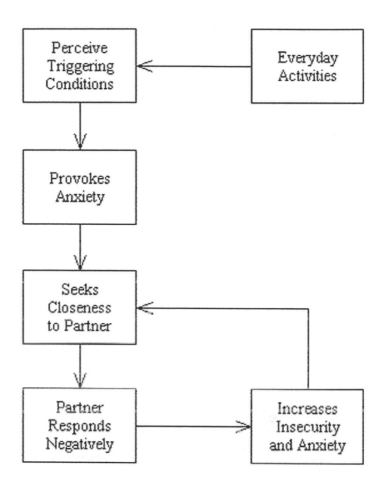

Here the partner asking for help or assurance gets either no response or a negative response—the other partner either fails to message back or sends a message refusing support. For example, the partner seeking assurance moves closer and tries for a hug, but the declining partner gets up and leaves. Or a direct statement asking for help ("I need you to go with me to the nursery so we can pick out some new plants") is met by rejection ("I don't have time to go with you since I have to pick up your brat after his soccer practice.") The response in this case increases anxiety and leads to more insistent messages asking for support; the requester is anxious and the decliner has even more reason to see themselves as put-upon by the requester's demands. If this cycle repeats too often, the attachment will weaken and the next strategy, attachment-avoidance, will be used.

This is flowchart for the **attachment-avoidance** strategy:

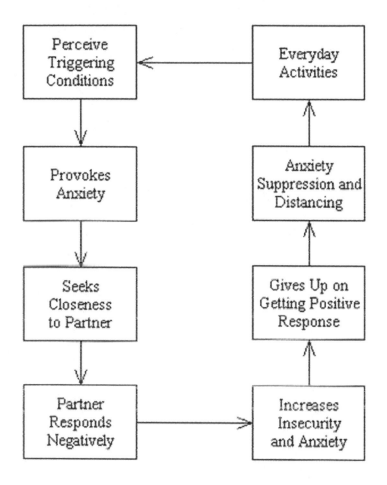

Here the partner requesting assurance handles rejection by *distancing*—lowering their expectations of support from the other partner. This pattern shows the breakdown of the request-assurance system and if predominant ultimately results in a broken or unhappy relationship. Note that nothing is inherently good or bad about any of these patterns, and all relationships have moments in the less secure loops - but a couple which spends most of its time cycling through the hyperactivation or attachment-avoidance message cycles is not likely to feel happy and secure in their relationship.

PART TWO

ATTACHMENT TYPES

How we treat others in close relationships depends on our *attachment style*. Researchers in child development in the 1940s examined the emotional damage done to orphans and displaced children; out of that and further research in childhood development in the 1960s came the field now called *attachment theory*.[6]

Children learn from their caregivers how to call for help and how to get their basic needs met through communication. A highly responsive caregiver who is good at understanding the child's state and responding as needed tends to encourage the child's trust in the caregiver and an attitude of safety in the world that encourages exploration and play, because the child feels secure—if he or she gets into trouble and cries out for help, the caregiver will come and save them. On the other hand, a child whose needs are ignored, or inconsistently met, or who is abused, develops a whole set of different adaptations to survive—some of which form the background assumptions to how they emotionally view the world of other people.

For a thorough discussion of the development and basics of adult attachment theory, read the Wikipedia entry "Attachment in Adults" and the seminal Hazan and Shaver paper, "Romantic Love Conceptualized as an Attachment Process."[7]

CHAPTER FOUR

WHAT IS ATTACHMENT TYPE?

Studies have shown that the styles of dealing with caregivers —those most important giants who kept us safe and fed during childhood—tend to carry on in adulthood, and the basic templates adopted then are used to deal with anyone close—partners or friends. Knowing what templates we use, and the templates others use with us, can give us an intellectual understanding of communications issues that allows us to empathize with partners who are driving us crazy with their neediness, or hurting us with their coldness —it's all in the signal-response dynamics of our attachment style. In this book a person will be categorized by their predominant attachment style by referring to their *attachment type.*

CHAPTER FIVE

WHAT TYPE ARE YOU?

First we'll look at your attachment type—which will suggest what type of partner will be good for you, and whether you yourself have some attachment issues you can address to be a better partner to others.

There's a more accurate and self-scoring test developed by S. Chris Fraley[8] online, so if you have access to the web while reading this, go take his test now at http://goo.gl/U9rNv and skip the one here

Answer each of the following questions to the best of your ability, not taking too long to think about it. If you currently have a romantic partner, imagine he or she is the other person you're being asked about; if not, answer as as if you're being asked about close friends or loved ones you have known.

For each statement, circle the number that corresponds to your feeling about that statement.

4 means you Strongly Agree.
3 means you Agree.

2 means you feel Neutral, or the statement is Not Applicable.

1 means you Disagree.

0 means you Strongly Disagree.

1. My desire to be very close sometimes scares people away.	0	1	2	3	4
2. I find it easy to trust other people.	0	1	2	3	4
3. I often worry about being abandoned.	0	1	2	3	4
4. I usually discuss my problems and concerns with people close to me.	0	1	2	3	4
5. Sometimes I think that other people don't really like me.	0	1	2	3	4
6. I am very comfortable being close to people.	0	1	2	3	4
7. Sometimes I'm afraid that if people really knew me, they wouldn't like me.	0	1	2	3	4
8. I like sharing my private thoughts and feelings with people close to me.	0	1	2	3	4
9. If I really love someone, I worry that they might meet someone else they like better.	0	1	2	3	4
10. I find it easy to depend on others.	0	1	2	3	4
11. If I show my feelings for someone, I worry they might not feel the same about me.	0	1	2	3	4
12. I would tell my romantic partner just about everything.	0	1	2	3	4
13. People often don't want to get as close as I would like.	0	1	2	3	4
14. I have no problem showing people how I feel deep down.	0	1	2	3	4
15. I worry a lot about my relationships.	0	1	2	3	4
16. The closer I get to someone, the more comfortable I feel with him or her.	0	1	2	3	4
17. I secretly worry about my friends or partners leaving me.	0	1	2	3	4
18. People close to me really seem to understand me and my needs.	0	1	2	3	4

Add your answers on 1, 3, 5, 7, 9, 11, 13, 15, and 17 =
This is your Anxiety score, from 0 to 36

Add your answers on 2, 4, 6, 8, 10, 12, 14, 16, and 18 =
This is your Closeness score, from 0 to 36.

If both your scores are below 18, you are a **Dismissive-Avoidant** attachment type.

If your Anxiety score is 18 or more and your Closeness score is less than 18, you are a **Fearful-Avoidant** attachment type.

If your Anxiety score is less than 18 and your Closeness score is 18 or more, you are a **Secure** attachment type.

If both your Anxiety score and Closeness score are 18 or more, you are an **Anxious-Preoccupied** type.

You will notice if you retake this test thinking of a different relationship than your current one, or imagining a relationship with a too-clingy or too-distancing partner, the relationship you are thinking of can strongly influence the attachment type you appear to be. "The idea is that when we're with a noncommittal person who's always threatening to leave, we're prone to feel like a clingy, ambivalent child— regardless of our previous attachment experience. When we're with an insecure, punishing nag, we're prone to become somewhat distant and avoidant."[9]

So, while one tends to have a predominant attachment style from childhood experiences, how you behave in a real relationship may vary as the style of your partner influences you. All of us have secure and insecure moments and can temporarily or under stress exhibit any of the patterns.

Chapter Six

Self-Esteem

In simplest form, the attachment types (predominant attachment styles) can be seen as the results of thoughts about self-esteem versus thoughts about the value of sociability with others, especially with respect to intimacy.

Those who have positive thoughts about sociability and so value and trust intimacy with others are *secure* (if they have positive self-esteem—that is, believe themselves to be worthy)—or, (if they have negative self-esteem, and so are anxious about the evaluations of others) *anxious-preoccupied.*

Those who have negative thoughts of sociability (thoughts about others) are *avoidant*—so-named because they avoid intimacy, and can either be *dismissive-avoidant* (if they have positive self-esteem—that is, believe themselves worthy enough to do without the support of close relationships) or *fearful-avoidant* (if they have low self-esteem—that is, they believe others will reject them in a close relationship.) Both avoidant types avoid intimacy because they think others are untrustworthy, or are afraid of intimacy because they think they will be rejected if fully known. The key difference between the avoidant subtypes is apparent positive self-esteem among the dismissive-avoidant, who seem to have adopted the attitude that they don't like or need intimacy, and negative self-esteem in the fearful-avoidant, who (while sometimes desiring intimacy as an ideal) are too afraid of it in reality to feel safe in a close relationship.

		Self-esteem thoughts about self	
		Positive	Negative
Sociability thoughts about others	Positive	Secure	Anxious–preoccupied
	Negative	Dismissive–avoidant	Fearful–avoidant

It might seem ideal if every person had high self-esteem, but like a person's judgments about others, evaluations of the self are only as valuable as they are accurate. A person who (wrongly) expects everyone to do him wrong is blind to the real allies he has in the world, while a person who thinks he is capable of far more than he actually is (and blames everyone else for his problems) will make bad decisions in the real world. A *realistic* level of self-esteem, accompanied by the skills of empathy and honest communication, is ideal.

> [High self-esteem] increases initiative, probably because it lends confidence. People with high self-esteem are more willing to act on their beliefs, to stand up for what they believe in, to approach others, to risk new undertakings. (This unfortunately includes being extra willing to do stupid or destructive things, even when everyone else advises against them.)...It can also lead people to ignore sensible advice as they stubbornly keep wasting time and money on hopeless causes.[10]

Nathaniel Branden defines *self-esteem* as "the experience of being competent to cope with the basic challenges of life and being worthy of happiness." Self-esteem has components of self-confidence (a feeling of personal capacity) and self-respect (a feeling of personal worth).

Maslow's well-known hierarchy of needs includes a need for esteem, which includes attitudes toward the self (confidence, self-esteem, achievement) and social esteem, (positive attitudes toward others as well as the respect and admiration of others gained through achievement.) The healthiest expression of self-esteem is based not on flattery or egotism, but real achievements and the regard of friends, family, and co workers.

Maslow's Pyramid of Needs[11]

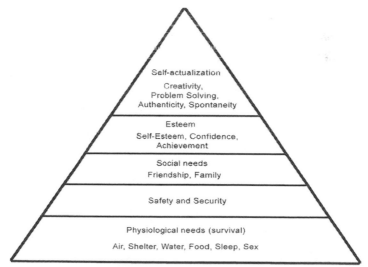

CHAPTER SEVEN

SECURE

A person of the secure attachment type (who we will call a *Secure*) is self-confident, empathetic, and observant of the feelings of others. Having been brought up with responsive caregivers and feeling safe in relying on others for comfort and care, the secure person has confidence that she can be herself and disclose her own inner thoughts and feelings to those close to her without fear of rejection—and when she is rejected by someone unfamiliar, know that she is worthwhile and not feel much hurt by others' moods and negative feelings. Confident of her worth, she can roam the emotional world freely and assist others with her strength and empathy; lacking the fears and preoccupations of the other types, she can communicate honestly, empathize completely, and love unconditionally.

How did these people reach their secure state? Some children seem to be naturally resilient, and will find enough good caregivers even in a less-than-ideal childhood to overcome, say, a negligent mother. Others not born with a secure predisposition may achieve it by the attention of responsive but not overbearing parents. And yet others grow into a secure style in adulthood by overcoming their initial, less functional attachment type through therapy, introspection and study, or (most commonly) a significant centering relationship with a partner or a community of friends.

It is the ability to "see" into the feelings of others that separates the secure type most from the others. A quiet, calm attachment center allows the secure person to attune themselves to others, making them better parents, partners, friends, and employees. And the ability to freely express both positive and negative feelings enhances their relationships. This is the skill called *emotional intelligence.*[12]

> If the secure adults had unhappy attachment histories, they seem to have understood and worked them through, at least to the extent that they could speak about them without getting into a stew, often demonstrating insight into the effects their negative experiences had had on them as well as some forgiveness or understanding of the parent's behavior.[13]

> Both Fonagy and Main believe that the most important quality distinguishing the secure from the anxious adults is their capacity to understand what makes themselves and others tick. They are better able to recognize their own inner conflicts and to have a sense of why their parents behaved as they did.[14]

The benefits of the secure style accumulate over a lifetime. Secure children are more liked and have more friends than others, and tend to have happier family lives.

> Kobak found that secure teens—those who were able to speak coherently and thoughtfully about their experiences

with their parents—were better able to handle conflicts with both mother and father. They were more assertive and more capable of listening to their parents' point of view. And they showed less dysfunctional, critical anger. They also made an easier transition to college.[15]

Secures find partners and friends more easily, form attachment bonds more readily, and tend to have longer and happier marriages.

In working with others, Secures use their ability to reflect on their own (and others') inner emotional states to more effectively communicate. Their emotional intelligence lets them work in teams, understand the emotional messages sent by others and respond appropriately, both verbally and nonverbally—others understand their feelings better and have a greater sense they can be relied on. Thus, on the whole, Secures are more successful in a group work environment. Secures also have higher incomes, on average.

If you are dating a Secure, he puts his cards on the table, and will show interest if interested, or decline to go forward if not. Secure people don't withhold or manipulate to get what they want—they tell you what they want, and offer what they have to give freely once a relationship is underway. A Secure wants you integrated into his life—he wants his friends and family to be your friends and family, if possible. A Secure does not try to keep you from knowing them, or live a compartmentalized life where you are not welcome in some settings, like work or family. When there is conflict in goals or plans, the Secure will make an effort to understand your point of view and find a compromise that satisfies you both.

A Secure does not put up barriers or constantly talk of "boundaries"—if you press on him too hard, the Secure will let you know your error, but not hold it against you. A Secure can speak freely about his feelings and memories, and explain how he feels or felt so you can understand it, and he values your understanding of who he is and how he got to be that way. Secure people tend to show anger in a relationship more easily, but quickly recover their calm and don't hold grudges —someone who is honestly angry at you for a good reason is communicating their distress in a healthy way, when a less secure type might suppress it and add to a secret store of resentments you will never be told about directly.

Levine and Heller have a nice list of the ideal characteristics of Secures:

- Great conflict busters—During a fight they don't feel the need to act defensively or to injure or punish their partner, and so prevent the situation from escalating.
- Mentally flexible—They are not threatened by criticism. They're willing to reconsider their ways, and if necessary, revise their beliefs and strategies.
- Effective communicators—They expect others to be understanding and responsive, so expressing their feelings freely and accurately to their partners comes naturally to them.
- Not game players—They want closeness and believe others want the same, so why play games?
- Comfortable with closeness, unconcerned about boundaries—They seek intimacy and aren't afraid of

being "enmeshed." Because they aren't overwhelmed by a fear of being slighted (as are the anxious) or the need to deactivate (as are the avoidants), they find it easy to enjoy closeness, whether physical or emotional.

- Quick to forgive—They assume their partners' intentions are good and are therefore likely to forgive them when they do something hurtful.
- Inclined to view sex and emotional intimacy as one —They don't need to create distance by separating the two (by being close either emotionally or sexually but not both).
- Treat their partners like royalty—When you've become part of their inner circle, they treat you with love and respect.
- Secure in their power to improve the relationship— They are confident in their positive beliefs about themselves and others, which makes this assumption logical.
- Responsible for their partners' well-being—They expect others to be responsive and loving toward them and so are responsive to others' needs.[10]

Roughly half of the population is secure, but since Secures are more successful at getting into and maintaining happy relationships, Secures are less and less available in older dating pools.

CHAPTER EIGHT

ANXIOUS-PREOCCUPIED

People of the anxious-preoccupied type (who we will call the *Preoccupied*) are the third-largest attachment type group, at about 20% of the population. Because their early attachment needs were unsatisfied or inconsistently satisfied, they crave intimacy but tend to feel doubtful about their own worth, making it harder for them to trust that they are loved and cared for. At the extremes, and with a more secure or dismissive partner, they are viewed as "needy" or "clingy," and can drive others away by their demands for attention. Many have never been able to come to terms with memories of parental failures:

> Often they spoke as if the feelings of hurt and anger they had as children were as alive in them today as they had been twenty or thirty years before. The childhoods they described were often characterized by intense efforts to please their parents, considerable anger and disappointment, and by role reversals in which the child had tried to parent the adult. But these memories were expressed in a confused and incoherent manner, as if they had never been able to get a grip on what happened to them and integrate it into a comprehensible picture. They seemed still so enmeshed with their parents that infantile

feelings flooded and bewildered them as they recalled the past.[17]

Unable to bring their adult understandings to the disappointments of their childhood, they may have created a falsely glowing story to bury the pain of feeling unappreciated:

> Anxious adults either failed to have insights into themselves and their parents or offered explanations that were platitudinous, self-deceptive, or self-serving. Thus one anxious [woman], when asked about the relationship between her parents, responded: "I am the apple of my father's eye and... he does absolutely idolize me... and I think it's amazing that my mother has never been remotely jealous of me in any way at all!"[18]

This insecurity is often the result of an insecure parental figure who is herself too needy to allow her child independence with assurance:

> A mother who has never worked through her own ambivalent attachment has probably been struggling all her life to find stable love. When she was a child, she may have been pained by the competent, steady caring that she saw friends' parents give to them. As an adult she may be prone to a nagging, uncontrollable jealousy in any close relationships, where she feels cause for doubt. She may want to love deeply and steadily, but it is hard for her because she's never been filled up enough with patient, reliable love to be in a position to give it.... Some preoccupied mothers frequently intrude when the baby is happily exploring on his own and push for interaction

even when the baby resists it.... For if a mother unconsciously wishes to keep a baby addicted to her, there is no better strategy than being inconsistently available. Nothing makes a laboratory rat push a pedal more furiously than an inconsistent reward.

The immature, dependent, babyish behavior that Sroufe observed in some ambivalent children may, thus, represent the sort of child his [preoccupied] parent unconsciously wishes for, who will not grow up and separate from mom, who will always be clingy demonstrating his need for her, and who will anxiously seek to appease her. The child, meanwhile, suspended perpetually in his attachment anxieties may, if he gets stuck in his mother's orbit, grow into a similar sort of person, who constantly seeks succor and devotion from another—much more than the average person is likely to put up with.[19]

As preoccupied children grow up, others notice they are too self-centered to quietly listen to emotional messages sent by others, and likely to be unreliable partners in games or work, as in this assessment by fellow students:

The preoccupied students—embroiled, angry, and incoherent when speaking about their parents—"were seen by their peers as more anxious, introspective, ruminative."[20]

Since they require constant messages of reassurance, the preoccupied find it hard to venture away from their partners or loved ones to accomplish goals, and will undermine their partners if necessary to keep their attention for themselves. The classic clingy child or parent or partner is acting out their anxiety about abandonment:

> [The preoccupied] are hypervigilant about separations, likely to become anxious or even panicky when left, and to be overcome by feelings of clinginess and impotent rage. They do not readily venture forth or take chances, for they do not believe their attachment needs will ever be met. They cling tenaciously to what they have, often using guilt and blame to keep their attachment figures on a short leash.[21]

> Anxious [preoccupied] children learn to manipulate to get their needs met, and invariably their manipulations get carried over into adulthood. The child may become seductive or cute, act fretful, or make others feel guilty for not giving him the attention he wants, all depending on the what strategic styles are modeled or succeed in the family.[22]

In Hazan and Shaver's study, preoccupied adults in a work setting "tended to procrastinate, had difficulty concentrating, and were most distracted by interpersonal concerns. They also had the lowest average income."[23] This inability to concentrate on anything but relationships handicaps the preoccupied, and makes them trouble for teams where they will put their need for reassurance ahead of the task at hand. As team members, the preoccupied require more management time and attention, and produce less work.

In dating, the preoccupied put their best foot forward and try too hard, sometimes missing the subtle cues that would allow them to listen better to understand their partner's feelings. They feel they must always prove themselves and act to keep your interest—they want constant interaction, constant touch and reassurance, which other types can find maddening. As long as they are getting the attention they want, they will let their partner get away with being difficult in other ways—even negative attention is keeping the touch game going. If their relationships last, it is often because they have found a partner whose insecurities dovetail with theirs, who will participate in a dysfunctional game similar to what they were raised with. While the preoccupied have strong feelings and can discuss them when calm, their feelings are centered around their needs for attention and the failures of others to provide it on demand. They commonly blame others for not understanding their feelings and needs while not feeling safe enough in the relationship to describe them openly. They want to merge with their partner, so this type is prone to codependence—a dysfunctional mutual dependence where neither partner matures further. They are profoundly disturbed by and resist even short separations. The single Preoccupied badly wants a partner and spends a lot of time feeling lonely.

Further Reading

Love and Addiction[24] by Peele and Brodsky is an older but still valuable self-help book for those who have an unhealthy addiction to the idea of being "in love." For hints on how to look for a healthy relationship if you tend to be anxious-preoccupied, this blog post by Shepell is valuable: "Forming Healthy Relationships with an Anxious Attachment Style."[25] *Attached: The New Science of Adult Attachment and How It Can Help You Find—and Keep—Love*[26] by Levine and Heller has a lot of good advice for the preoccupied.

CHAPTER NINE

DISMISSIVE-AVOIDANT

Much of what follows also applies to the fearful-avoidant, who can be thought of as the avoidant who haven't given up. The term "avoidant" is used to discuss characteristics shared by both the dismissive-avoidant and the fearful-avoidant.

The two avoidant types (dismissive-avoidant and fearful-avoidant) share a subconscious fear that caregivers are not reliable and intimacy is a dangerous thing. The dismissive-avoidant individuals (who we will call *Dismissives*) have completed a mental transformation that says: "I am good, I don't need others, and they aren't really important to me. I am fine as I am," while the fearful-avoidant are still consciously craving an intimacy which scares them when it actually happens. Both types were trained not to rely on caregivers, but the Dismissive has dealt with this by deciding he doesn't need others much at all, and so has little apparent reason to participate in the emotional signaling of a close relationship.

Dismissives are rarely open about declaring themselves contemptuous of others. But they think highly of themselves and will tell you they value their self-sufficiency and independence—needing others is weak, feelings of attachment are strings that hold you down, empathy and sympathy are for lesser creatures.

A Dismissive often has a story of a previous relationship which was never fully realized or ended when his partner left —early in his romantic life, or perhaps long-distance. The memory of this idealized previous partner is used as a weapon when the Dismissive tires—as they quickly do—of a real relationship and its demands; no one could measure up to the one that got away. This is another distancing trick to keep real intimacy at bay.

Dismissives have poor access to early emotional memories, having built a defensive shield of self-esteem and self-sufficiency that requires negative memories to be suppressed:

> Adults characterized as "dismissing of attachment" seemed unable or unwilling to take attachment issues seriously. They answered questions in a guarded way, without much elaboration, and often had trouble remembering their childhoods. They seemed to dislike and distrust looking inward. Some exhibited an underlying animosity that seemed to imply: "Why are you asking me to dredge up this stuff?" or "The whole point of this interview is stupid!" The dismissing adults spoke vaguely about their parents, frequently describing them in idealized terms. But when pressed for incidents that might illustrate such descriptions, their memories contradicted their assessments, as negative facts leaked into their narratives. Thus, one [dismissive] called his mother "nice" but eventually revealed that she was often drunk and swore at him. When asked if that bothered him, he replied, "Not at

all. That's what made me the strong person I am today. I'm not like those people at work who have to hold [each other's] hands before making a decision."

This stalwart, anti-sniveling response was typical of the way dismissing subjects played down the affect of early hurts or embraced them as having built their character. Another [dismissive] described his mother as "loving," "caring," "the world's most affectionate person," "invariably available to her children," "an institution." But pressed for details, he could not recall a single instance of his mother's warmth or nurturance.[27]

Fellow students recognized the hostility and mistrust of the dismissive:

The dismissing freshmen—who had trouble remembering early experiences with their parents and played down the importance of attachments issues in their interviews —"were seen by their peers as more hostile, more condescending, more distant."[28]

The buried need for emotional attachment is not consciously felt by dismissives, but their need for others can show itself unconsciously:

If a spouse is away for a period of time, it is natural to miss him. If a move is made to a new place, it is natural to feel a loss over friends and family who have been left behind and to work assiduously to create new ties to replace the old. But with separations, too, anxious attachment can deform the process. Clinical work suggests that people with what appears to be an avoidant or dismissive psychology often fail to recognize that separations have an emotional impact in them. ... When a spouse is away, a person with this psychology may become obsessively focused on work, may even celebrate the separation as an opportunity to get more work done, but then be strangely, perhaps even cruelly distant from the spouse when he or she returns.[29]

Dismissives will learn to get their needs for attention, sex, and community met through less demanding partners who fail to require real reciprocation or intimacy (often the anxious-preoccupied!):

An avoidantly attached boy ... will probably learn to disguise his care seeking, He may become adept at using various forms of control to get another person to be there for him; he may seek out people whose needs are more apparent and who give without having to be asked.[30]

Avoidants "were most likely to be workaholics and most inclined to allow work to interfere with social life. Some said they worked too hard to have time for socializing, others that they preferred to work alone. Not surprisingly, their incomes were as high as the secures, but their satisfaction was as low as [the preoccupied.]"[31] Because of their ability to focus on work and act independently, dismissives can be phenomenal explorers and individual contributors. In fields where performance is not based on group efforts, and a lack of concern for others' feelings can actually be beneficial, the dismissive can be a star player—for example, in some types of litigation, or some scientific fields.

In dating, avoidants can be charming and have learned all the social graces—they often know how they are expected to act in courtship and can play the role well for a time. But lacking a positive view of attached others, they expect relationships to fulfill a romantic ideal which no real human being can create for them, so all fall short and are discarded when it becomes inconvenient to continue. Typically as the relationship ages, avoidants will begin to find fault and focus on petty shortcomings of their partner. Because they are not really aware of their own feelings, they can't talk about them in a meaningful way, and often the first clue the about-to-be-dumped have that something is wrong is the avoidant's move to break up with them. Once you have read this book, you will likely be aware of the missing signals and the many small clues that the avoidant is not committing to you or anyone any time soon, but those who are unaware of this type will usually soldier on, not trusting their own feeling that something about Prince Charming is not quite right.

The dismissive-avoidant is afraid of and incapable of tolerating true intimacy. Since he was brought up not to depend on anyone or reveal feelings that might not be acceptable to caregivers, his first instinct when someone gets really close to him is to run away. Superficially the dismissive (as opposed to the fearful-avoidant) thinks very highly of himself, and is likely to pin any blame for relationship troubles on his partners; but underneath (especially in the extreme form we label narcissism), there is such low self esteem that at his core he does not feel his true self is worthy of love and attention. Should a partner penetrate his armor, unconscious alarm bells go off and he retreats to either aloneness or the safety of companionship with others who do not realize he is not what he appears to be on the surface.

The dismissive attempts to limit his level of exposure to partners by manipulating his response, commonly by failing to respond to messages requesting assurance. Dismissives let you know that you are low on their priority list, and your inner emotional state is your problem—when you are with one, you are really still alone, in an attachment sense. By only partly participating in the normal message-response of the attached, they subconsciously limit the threat another poses to their independence. This behavior is called *distancing*, and all of us do it to limit our intimacy with others when we don't want to be as close as they do, but for the dismissive it's a tool to be used on the most important people in their lives.

Levine and Heller have a useful list of distancing behaviors (also called deactivating strategies):

• Saying (or thinking) "I'm not ready to commit"—but staying together nonetheless, sometimes for years.
• Focusing on small imperfections in your partner: the way s/he talks, dresses, eats, or (fill in the blank) and allowing it to get in the way of your romantic feelings.
• Pining after an ex-girlfriend/ boyfriend—(the "phantom ex"— more on this later).
• Flirting with others—a hurtful way to introduce insecurity into the relationship.
• Not saying "I love you"—while implying that you do have feelings toward the other person.
• Pulling away when things are going well (e.g., not calling for several days after an intimate date).

- Forming relationships with an impossible future, such as with someone who is married.
- "Checking out mentally" when your partner is talking to you.
- Keeping secrets and leaving things foggy—to maintain your feeling of independence.
- Avoiding physical closeness—e.g., not wanting to share the same bed, not wanting to have sex, walking several strides ahead of your partner."

The more extreme avoidants are almost incapable of talking about their feelings; whatever feelings they do have access to are primarily negative and they have great difficulty describing them verbally.

This syndrome is called *alexithymia*", the roots of the word literally meaning "having no words for feelings," which is not at all the same thing as not having feelings. The worst cases can only express themselves with inchoate rages and tantrums, or unexplained physical symptoms like stomach pains and adrenalin rushes.

The most compelling theory of how consciousness arose has between-person communication (primitive language) giving rise to internal communication, so that what we see as a stream of consciousness is actually internal dialogue, talking to yourself. Noting this, you might say that an inability to name and talk about feelings cripples a person's ability to be consciously aware of them. If one is very poor at doing this, one would tend to note feelings only as manifested in somatic symptoms like fast heart rate, discomfort, loss of energy, nervousness, etc.

This is why talking to someone about how you feel (or writing about it) is also training for being conscious of feelings internally. The more you talk about it to others, the more you can talk about it to yourself. Even for those not suffering from alexithymia, talking or writing about feelings can clarify understanding of them, which is one of the reasons talk therapy is effective.

Further Reading

For the most severe cases, read Kantor, Martin. *Distancing: Avoidant Personality Disorder, Revised and Expanded.*[34] There is some literature online gently warning of the difficulty of changing the avoidant types, for example: "Q&A: Can I Change Someone with an Avoidant Attachment Style?"[35]

CHAPTER TEN

FEARFUL-AVOIDANT

The fearful-avoidant (sometimes called anxious-avoidant) share an underlying distrust of caregiving others with the dismissive-avoidant, but have not developed the armor of high self-esteem to allow them to do without attachment; they realize the need for and want intimacy, but when they are in a relationship that starts to get close, their fear and mistrust surfaces and they distance. In psychology this is called an approach-avoidance conflict[36]; at a distance the sufferer wants to get closer, but when he does, the fear kicks in and he wants to withdraw. This leads to a pattern of circling or cycling, and the fearful-avoidant can often be found in a series of short relationships ended by their finding fault with a partner who seems more threatening as the partner gets closer to understanding.

The early caregiving of a fearful-avoidant type often has some features of both neglect and abuse (which may be psychological—a demeaning or absent caregiver, rejection and teasing from early playmates.) A fearful-avoidant type both desires close relationships and finds it difficult to be truly open to intimacy with others out of fear of rejection and loss, since that is what he or she has received from caregivers.

Instead of the dismissive's defense mechanism of going it alone and covering up feelings of need for others by developing high self-esteem, the fearful-avoidant subconsciously believe there is something unacceptable about them that makes anyone who knows them deeply likely to reject or betray them, so they will find reasons to relieve this fear by distancing anyone who gets too close. As with the dismissive, the fearful-avoidant will have difficulty understanding the emotional lives of others, and empathy, while present, is not very strong—thus there will be poor communication of feelings with his partner.

> Both Ainsworth and Main found the mother of the avoidant child to be distant—rejecting of the infant's attachment needs, hostile to signs of dependency, and disliking affectionate, face-to-face physical contact, especially when the baby desired it. Her aversion to nurturance would seem to be a logical outgrowth of the neglect she probably experienced when she herself was young. Needs and longings that were painfully unmet have become a source of hurt and shame for her. Having cut herself off from them, they make her angry, depressed, or disgusted when she sees them in her child.[37]

A narcissistic or demanding mother can cause a child to mold him- or herself to please the parent to the point where little remains of the child's own feelings and personality; they have been trained to display a false personality to gain parental approval.

Children who have been brought up this way often become high-achieving, competent adults with a sense of hollowness at the core, and episodic low self-esteem. They are often from families where parents are highly competent and have high expectations, and parenting may have been so active that childhood selves were quashed by parental expectations, judgments, and signals. In other words, parental ego is so dominant that the child's true feelings are buried to avoid their disapproval. What the child learns to display is a false persona more pleasing to the active and admired parents. Some authors, notably Alice Miller, have called such parenting "abuse," though it is abuse through disapproval and verbal rejection of behavior the caregiver disliked.[30]

While we all have public faces versions of ourselves edited for public consumption—the fearful-avoidant have commonly developed a *false self*, an acceptable outer personality which inhibits spontaneous display of their innermost thoughts and feelings even in intimacy. Those who think of themselves as their friends will often be surprised and hurt when high stress brings out the true personality of the masked one. By hiding their true selves, such people live with a social support network that has been attracted by their fake persona, so that when a crisis occurs, those who might have cared for them aren't around, and those who are around don't care for the real person revealed by the crisis. In a quotation commonly misattributed to Dr. Seuss (but actually a modified quote from Bernard Baruch), "Be who you are and say what you feel, because those who mind don't matter and those who matter don't mind." Real intimacy and loyalty are founded on honesty, and pretending to be someone you aren't—keeping up appearances—leaves you with no lasting close friends or partners.

A fairy tale that is a parable for the warped attachment views of the avoidant:

> There was once a dreadfully wicked hobgoblin. One day he had a simply marvelous idea. He was going to make a looking glass that would reflect everything that was good and beautiful in such a way that it would look dreadful or at least not very important. When you looked in it, you would not be able to see any of the good or the beautiful in yourself or in the world. Instead, this looking glass would reflect everything that was bad or ugly and make it look very important. The most beautiful landscapes would look like heaps of garbage, and the best people would look repulsive or would seem stupid. People's faces would be so changed that they could not be recognized, and if there was anything that a person was ashamed of or wanted to hide, you could be sure that this would be just the thing that the looking glass emphasized.

> The hobgoblin set about making this looking glass, and when he was finished, he was delighted with what he had done. Anyone who looked into it could only see the bad and the ugly, and all that was good and beautiful in the world was distorted beyond recognition.

> One day the hobgoblin's assistants decided to carry the looking glass up to the heavens so that even the angels would look into it and see themselves as ugly and stupid. They hoped that perhaps even God himself would look into it! But, as they reached the heavens, a great invisible force stopped them and they dropped the dreadful looking glass. And as it fell, it broke into millions of pieces.

And now came the greatest misfortune of all. Each of the pieces was hardly as large as a grain of sand, and they flew about all over the world. If anyone got a bit of glass in his eye there it stayed, and then he would see everything as ugly or distressing. Everything good would look stupid. For every tiny splinter of the glass possessed the same power that the whole glass had!

Some people got a splinter in their hearts, and that was dreadful, too, for then their hearts turned into lumps of ice and could no longer feel love.

The hobgoblin watched all this and he laughed until his sides ached. And still the tiny bits of glass flew about, And now we will hear all about it.... —from The Snow Queen, Hans Christian Andersen

PART THREE

THE SCARY MONSTERS

We've looked at the basic attachment styles—all of these are normal behaviors exhibited by apparently well-adjusted citizens in our society, and it's possible (although perhaps not optimal) to have a long-term relationship with any of them. Now we're going to discuss the scarier monsters—psychopaths and the dangerously unbalanced you may meet out there. These people are at the extreme fringes of the attachment styles, or are lacking some of the qualities that make someone a member of a functioning society. While they may be apparently functional (studies show that corporate CEOs score high in psychopathic tendencies!), you don't want to be close to one.

CHAPTER ELEVEN

SUBPERSONALITIES

In the discussion of the fearful-avoidant attachment type we mentioned the damage done by overly-perfectionist, narcissistic caregivers in causing children to suppress their true inner selves in favor of a false personality designed to please parents. Many of these children, as adults, have an inner voice which tends to find fault in themselves and others, an *inner critic.*[39]

This inner critic is an example of a *subpersonality*[40]—an inner persona with a distinctive voice and behavior, often learned from a caregiver or authority figure. Years of early childhood spent interacting with a person creates a model in a child's head of how that person would acts or speaks while observing the child's behavior, so the common observation that our parents live on in a sense as voices in our head is often correct. If we are brought up with love and attention, these voices are loving and positive, and guide us to confidence and achievement; if they are critical and negative, our view of the world, ourselves, and other people becomes unrealistically dark. Subpersonalities often come into play as defense mechanisms, shielding an abused child from the psychic damage poor treatment would otherwise produce.

Everyone's heard of *split personality*, formerly diagnosed as multiple personality disorder. Split personality (now diagnosed as *dissociative personality disorder*) occurs when abuse has been so extreme that these subpersonalities take on an independent character, almost as if another person or people are timesharing the same body. These cases are very rare and usually not as extreme as portrayed in popular culture. But everyone has subpersonalities—a more benign example would be the doctor's professional persona, where her voice and personality change so that she can behave as befits her work.

An alternative way of explaining the behavior of the avoidant is that they have a strong protective subpersonality that takes over at an unconscious level whenever intimacy gets too deep and a threat of pain or loss is perceived. The nonverbal, guardian protector subpersonality causes the avoidant to rationalize as much as necessary at a conscious level to justify actions distancing the threat; in other words, the avoidant acts to damage a relationship he may consciously believe he cares about.

The reason psychopaths and other dangerous characters can survive undetected in our society is that they have developed subpersonalities tailored to let them pass as normal. An intelligent, motivated psychopath can create a civilized subpersonality that in almost all situations lets him behave as normal, since the rules of behavior can be understood and applied without the empathy that reinforces them in most people.[41]

CHAPTER TWELVE

ABUSIVE NARCISSIST

Extreme versions of the attachment types can be diagnosed in adults as disorders. Many theorists believe that an entrenched avoidant attachment is at the core of the narcissistic personality disorder.[42]

Narcissism to varying degrees is a normal personality trait—we could substitute "self-centered" for the term and be correct. Psychologists think youthful narcissism is a part of typical emotional development—the stage where you say "Mine!" when asked about any toy. Normal children grow out of this as they experience the evaluations of others, and create a more realistic view of themselves and others as they grow up.

Many high-achieving adults score high on a narcissism test, being preoccupied with how they look to the world and working hard to increase the admiration received from others. In many professions this can be a useful and even necessary trait. But the most effective of them also understand and value the feelings of others, and thus are more *successfully* manipulative in getting them to do their bidding.

When we talk about dysfunctional narcissism, we are talking about adults whose self-centeredness and use of others to satisfy a deep need to be the center of attention has gone beyond functional to become abusive. The harm they do to their partners comes from manipulation, verbal and physical abuse, and abandonment—because the attention of a partner is only valued when it is shiny and new, and the increasing distress of a narcissist's partner is met with hostility instead of efforts to reassure. The narcissist has little empathy or sympathy for the feelings of others since he or she is only concerned about getting the attention needed to cover up the hollowness of their low self-esteem.

How does the narcissist get that way? As a defense to caregiving that devalues the child's true self, often provided by a narcissistic caregiver who needs the child to be "perfect" and "special" because that is how the caregiver views herself.

> Babies crave having their performance validated, they need to be seen and loved for who they truly are, and they need to be given an ongoing sense of belonging, of being a valued fellow being in the family. If a mother fails consistently to attune to her baby in this way and to respond to his complex emotional needs, the young child, feeling unknown and unappreciated, is unable to know or appreciate himself. He shrinks back into a sense of helplessness, smallness, defectiveness, and shame, which he may then defend against by clinging to his infantile grandiosity, a grandiosity one or both of his parents may promote.... Outwardly self-important, prone to pomposity, self-adoration, and an annoying attitude of entitlement, he is haunted by a fragile self-esteem. His

friends complain he's only interested in talking about himself, his boss that he takes frustrations too personally, his neighbors that he's pushy and conceited.[43]

Narcissistic personalty disorder is a recognized diagnostic category defined by the DSM-IV-TR, with these symptoms:

- Expects to be recognized as superior and special, without superior accomplishments
- Expects constant attention, admiration, and positive reinforcement from others
- Envies others and believes others envy him/her
- Preoccupied with thoughts of great success, enormous attractiveness, power, intelligence
- Lacks the ability to empathize with the feelings or desires of others
- Is arrogant in attitudes and behavior
- Has expectations of special treatment that are unrealistic

Splitting is the defense mechanism narcissists use to save their fragile self-images from real-world negative evaluation. The self is grandiosely inflated and all which fails to reflect this false high self esteem is devalued, "splitting" the world into good self-and-adherents and bad everything else. "Other people are either manipulated as an extension of one's own self, who serve the sole role of giving admiration and approval, or they are seen as worthless (because they cannot collude with the narcissist's grandiosity)."[44]

Narcissists are users: they exploit others ruthlessly for their own needs, and as a result tend to have few or no long-term relationships, with shallow and utilitarian relationships predominant.

Because of their underlying lack of self-esteem and dependence on others, they are deeply hurt or angered by criticism or a lack of the attention they feel they deserve, imagining slights in the most minor incidents.[45] Not having a realistic understanding of the emotional states of others, constant reinforcement of their egos (called *narcissistic supply*) is required for them to remain stable. If a relationship partner is critical or fails to provide the needed supply of ego-boosting attention, the narcissist will go into a rage and devalue the partner, with physical or emotional abuse being a common control technique. Tearing down others makes the narcissist feel better about themselves, and one key to recognizing a narcissist quickly is a self-reported history of being involved almost entirely with unreliable, crazy, or otherwise defective partners. No relationship breakdown is ever the narcissist's fault!

Narcissists believe they are special and better than other people, and if the universe fails to confirm their belief as it becomes clear in later life that their grandiose expectations will remain unsatisfied, psychic collapse and depression can result. Narcissists rarely recognize any problem with their condition until depression and loss have made them desperate.

How to Recognize a Narcissist

A narcissist tends to talk about himself in glowing terms and denigrate or diminish others in his life; if your date mentions several previous partners and has something bad to say about all of them, he's probably a narcissist, because no relationship issue is ever his fault. Putting down others to feel superior is their thing.

The narcissist may have the outward trappings of success, but of all the types in this book, the narcissist is the most likely to be deeply in debt to keep up appearances. The car is leased, the teeth are capped, the successes they talk about are exaggerations. If no one you've met knows him well and you can't confirm his stories, beware.

In conversation, unwillingness to listen to you talking about your life and your feelings is a red flag. No matter how interesting he seems to be, if he doesn't show signs of caring about how you feel, don't get sucked in. Ask yourself why this person wants you around if they don't care to know your history, your feelings, your friends, and your family—is it because you make a great fashion accessory? Does he look more successful when you're with him?

Any hint of controlling behavior—extreme jealousy, paranoid accusations, the sense that you have to justify yourself constantly—is a red flag. Also note as signs: overreacting to mild criticism, rages and tantrums when questioned, denial of obvious facts and events you have witnessed, and frequent lies and evasions.

The Abusive Narcissist

The classic abusive partner is a narcissist. Using verbal and physical abuse to control and maintain his relationship with a partner treated as an accessory, a narcissist can spend years demeaning and abusing a partner who is locked into a co-dependence; commonly the partner has fallen into extreme dependence as the narcissist has manipulated his partner into cutting off relationships with friends and family who might help. The narcissist will at first build up a victim and treat the victim well, then devalue and abuse, and this can be cyclic—if about to actually lose their partner, they will pretend to feel remorse and behave more sensitively for just long enough to lull the victim into staying. A long-term relationship with an abusive narcissist can severely damage the victim's self-esteem, finances, and support network, leaving him or her with few resources to recover.

Be aware that some of the more attractive people you will meet are narcissists, and they are life-destroying in a long-term relationship. Run like hell if you meet one.

Further Reading

If you recognize your parental figures as narcissists and you would like some insight on how to deal with that, one good book is *Children of the Self-Absorbed: A Grown-Up's Guide to Getting over Narcissistic Parents* by Nina W. Brown. Being trapped in a relationship with an abusive narcissist is such a common problem that there are many good self-help books on the topic:

Narcissistic Lovers: How to Cope, Recover and Move On by

Cythia Zayn and Kevin Dibble, M.S.

Narcissists Exposed: 75 Things Narcissists Don't Want You to Know by Drew Keys

Psychopath Free: Recovering from Emotionally Abusive Relationships With Narcissists, Sociopaths, & Other Toxic People, by Peace

The Wizard of Oz and Other Narcissists: Coping with the One-Way Relationship in Work, Love, and Family by Eleanor Payson

Emotional Assault: Recognizing an Abusive Partner's Bag of Tricks by Lisa Kroulik

Surviving a Narcissist - The Path Forward by Lisa Scott

Malignant Self-Love: Narcissism Revisited, by Sam Vaknin and Lidija Rangelovska

Chapter Thirteen

Sadist

The classic sadist derives pleasure from inflicting pain on others. This is not to be confused with sexual sadism, where pain is inflicted as a sexual thrill; the garden-variety sadist is on a control and power trip. It makes him (it's usually a him) feel better to hurt others, in all sorts of ways. As in all other traits, it's normal to experience moments of sadistic pleasure, and a trace of controlled sadism is part of many normal personalities; the dysfunctional variety takes it to an extreme which does harm to himself and others around him. *The New York Times* discussing the sadists among us:

> In 2002, Dr. Paulhus and colleagues had proposed a cluster of traits they called the Dark Triad: narcissism, psychopathy, and Machiavellianism. The traits are present in many people not currently in jail or in therapy. "It's a taxonomy of personalities whom others rate as being obnoxious, people you deal with on an everyday basis," Dr. Paulus said. He has been investigating if everyday sadism should be added to the cluster—a Dark Tetrad. "Psychopaths want to get things from people and don't care about hurting them to do so," he said. "Yet sadists look for opportunities to hurt people, and prolong it for their own pleasure." Studies also indicate that sadists will

choose to hurt people without provocation, even if the act takes time and effort — the only reward being the pleasure of inflicting cruelty. Dr. Paulhus wanted to see whether a questionnaire could predict which participants would make a sadistic choice. Again, 71 psychology students rated statements from the Dark Triad scale, as well as new ones like, "I enjoy mocking losers to their face," "I enjoy hurting people," and "In car racing, it's the accidents I enjoy most."[46]

The DSM-III-R Criteria for Sadistic Personality Disorder are the following:

A) A pervasive pattern of cruel, demeaning and aggressive behavior, beginning by early adulthood, as indicated by the repeated occurrence of at least four of the following:

• Has used physical cruelty or violence for the purpose of establishing dominance in a relationship (not merely to achieve some noninterpersonal goal, such as striking someone in order to rob him or her)

• Humiliates or demeans people in the presence of others

• Has treated or disciplined someone under his or her control unusually harshly (e.g., a child, student, prisoner, or patient)

• Is amused by, or takes pleasure in, the psychological or physical suffering of others (including animals)

• Has lied for the purpose of harming or inflicting pain on others (not merely to achieve some other goal)

• Gets other people to do what he or she wants by frightening them (through intimidation or even terror)

• Restricts the autonomy of people with whom he or she has close relationship (e.g., will not let spouse leave the house unaccompanied or permit teenage daughter to attend social functions)

• Is fascinated by violence, weapons, martial arts, injury, or torture

B) The behavior in A has not been directed toward only one person (e.g., spouse, one child) and has not been solely for the purpose of sexual arousal (as in sexual sadism).[47]

The underlying goal of the sadist is to achieve power and control over his environment by degrading and hurting other beings. Sadists will be attracted to police and military work, though in those roles they are often seen as "bad cops" or "bad soldiers" because their desire to abuse others is less under rational control. As is true of many abusive types, sadists have often been abused in childhood and taught to enjoy hurting those weaker than themselves by a bullying parental figure. Genetics and minor brain damage may also play a role in some cases, since the "Dark Tetrad" of sadism, narcissism, Machiavellianism, and psychopathy tends to run in families.

> Sadists like to inflict pain because they find suffering, both corporeal and psychological, amusing. They torture animals and people because, to them, the sights and sounds of a creature writhing in agony are hilarious and pleasurable. Sadists go to great lengths to hurt others: they lie, deceive, commit crimes, and even make personal sacrifices merely so as to enjoy the cathartic moment of witnessing someone else's misery.

> Sadists are masters of abuse by proxy and ambient abuse. They terrorize and intimidate even their nearest and dearest into doing their bidding. They create an aura and atmosphere of unmitigated yet diffuse dread and

consternation. This they achieve by promulgating complex "rules of the house" that restrict the autonomy of their dependants (spouses, children, employees, patients, clients, etc.). They have the final word and are the ultimate law. They must be obeyed, no matter how arbitrary and senseless are their rulings and decisions.

Most sadists are fascinated by gore and violence. They are vicarious serial killers: they channel their homicidal urges in socially acceptable ways by "studying" and admiring historical figures such as Hitler, for instance. They love guns and other weapons, are fascinated by death, torture, and martial arts in all their forms.[48]

Note that a sadistic *subpersonality* is far more common, and when controlled by an empathetic intelligence can be a functional part of a person. The underground sexual practices of sadomasochism use infliction of and submission to pain as part of consensual sex, which when satisfying for both partners can be seen as just another signaling of attachment, as in the bestselling *50 Shades of Gray*.[49] Also note that many functional long-term relationships are characterized by periodic fighting and infliction of pain on both sides—the extent to which this is dysfunctional is as usual dependent on the degree and the damage involved. In some cultures this drama is considered normal and the partners would report they are generally happy with their relationships.

But unchecked by an emotionally intelligent governing personality, a sadist will inflict pain that goes beyond mere signaling, and such abuse will only be tolerated by a partner with a matching desire to be degraded and hurt. If you're dating a sadist, you will quickly discover it in his interactions with others. Don't think that you will be able to change him or get special treatment:

> It's dangerous to think there's any way to be truly safe in any kind of relationship with a sadistic-aggressive personality or immune from the effects of their abuse. Some folks tell themselves they have sufficient strength to endure the torment they experience. Others allow themselves to think that as long as they're appeasing their sadist, they're safe. But even though sadists have much more respect for strength than they do for perceived weakness, there's really no way to be completely safe with them or to be unaffected by the psychological damage they can inflict. And sometimes sadists develop a special fascination with a particular "target," taking a sense of "ownership" over that target and exacerbating the risk associated with trying to break free of their grip Moreover, sadists can have other aggressive personality traits as well, making them even more dangerous (sadistic predatory aggressives [alt: sadistic psychopaths] are without question the most dangerous people on the planet). So it's very important to recognize these personalities early on and do your very best to stay clear of them.[50]

CHAPTER FOURTEEN

PSYCHOPATH

While the sadist and abusive narcissist are less empathetic, the psychopath almost completely lacks concern for the feelings of others—the psychopath doesn't enjoy hurting people or require their admiration, and he is capable of predicting how others will feel as the result of his actions, but he just doesn't care whether others feel good or bad about him. Less clever psychopaths end up identified as criminals and are locked away, or end up in marginal lifestyles when their disregard for others leads to violence or fraud, but the truly dangerous ones you might meet in a normal social context are able to act the part of thoughtful human beings well enough to fool almost anyone.

Traits of the Psychopath

The PCL-R is a test used by mental heath workers to rate or diagnose psychopathic tendencies in prisons or other institutions. The psychopathic traits to be evaluated by the test are:

- Glib and superficial charm
- Grandiosity
- Need for stimulation

- Pathological lying
- Cunning and manipulative
- Lack of remorse
- Callousness
- Poor behavioral controls
- Impulsiveness
- Irresponsibility
- Denial
- Parasitic lifestyle
- Sexual promiscuity
- Early behavior problems
- Lack of realistic long-term goals
- Failure to accept responsibility for own actions
- Many short-term marital relationships
- Juvenile delinquency
- Revocation of conditional release
- Criminal versatility

Note the similarities to the narcissist. The difference is that the narcissist requires the positive attention of others and directs his efforts toward retaining it, while the psychopath makes his way through life unconcerned by such factors. Garden-variety narcissists are not serial killers or criminals, though not all psychopaths go down those paths, either. Studies show that psychopaths tend to have brain abnormalities (either inherited or as a result of trauma in early development) that affect their social feelings.

CEOs of major corporations tend to score high on psychopathic traits—this is because a willingness to ignore the feelings of those around you and set off on a risky path can actually be beneficial in directing a business. This does not mean that CEOs are commonly dangerous psychopaths; it may mean that successful politicians, attorneys, and CEOs are simply able to use a bit of the trait effectively, especially when combined with high emotional and general intelligence and skill at acting the part of a concerned leader while not feeling the pressure to make every voter or employee like them.[51]

The psychopath you might meet may appear suave and successful on the outside, and may even have a magnetic personality that is hard to resist—Charles Manson is the classic example of a charismatic psychopath who could attract followers and manipulate them into following his murderous orders. Or take Ted Bundy, who was able to successfully gain sympathy from his female victims to lure them to their deaths. Normally you can trust your intuitions about the approach of a handsome stranger, but the chilling thing about the psychopathic killer is his ability to send false signals of reassurance to gain your sympathy. Your mother was right—never go anywhere isolated to meet with a stranger. Always meet in public unless you know him well or he has social connections with people you know.

Neuroscientist James Fallon was working with brain scans of psychopaths as part of his research into brain abnormalities seen in Alzheimer's patients when he discovered that his own brain scan resembled those of the psychopaths. He wrote a fascinating book, *The Psychopath inside: A Neuroscientist's Personal Journey into the Dark Side of the Brain*, discussing the experience and why he thinks he can function reasonably well in society despite his tendencies.[52]

Chapter Fifteen

Histrionic Personality

From the Latin for actor, *histrionicus,* the histrionic personality is characterized by excessive drama, display, and acting out of emotions. At about 2% of the population and usually associated with women (80% of those diagnosed with histrionic personality disorder are female), these characters can be engaging and attractive but exhausting in their need to be the center of attention. Often flirtation and seduction are used as tools to gain attention, and histrionic women can run into trouble being seen as pass-around party girls or "teases." Examples of the type in fiction include Blanche in *A Streetcar Named Desire*, and Marilyn Monroe's seductive film persona. Manipulative and vulnerable by turns, a histrionic type is easy to feel sympathy for and tempts one to try to "rescue" them, but as an extreme form of the anxious-preoccupied attachment type, the histrionic woman (or man) is, like the narcissist, typically unable to achieve a secure, equal intimacy with others—the pressure of her need for attention is too great.

PRAISE ME is a useful mnemonic for the signs of *histrionic personality disorder* (HPD):

- Provocative (or seductive) behavior

- Relationships are considered more intimate than they actually are
- Attention-seeking
- Influenced easily
- Speech (style) wants to impress; lacks detail
- Emotional lability; shallowness
- Make-up; physical appearance is used to draw attention to self
- Exaggerated emotions; theatrical[53]

In less extreme forms, where the woman is seen as overly dramatic or hysterical but not so extreme as to be unable to function in a relationship, this can be charming to those who don't know her well:

> The live wire. Seductive and engaging, she can often make people feel there's no one on earth they'd rather be with. Often diagnosed as a hysterical character, she is scattered, charmingly incompetent, and easily thrown into a tizzy by schedules, details, and responsibilities. Her dramatic flair makes her popular. Male neighbors delight in meeting her in the hall, and they wonder: "Why is she married to him?" But she flees from intimacy, and like the ambivalent child, she tends to be demanding or clingy, immature, and easily overwhelmed by her own emotions.[54]

It's emotionally draining to maintain a relationship with such a needy person, and it's often a caretaking arrangement, with the stable partner smoothing out the difficulties of the real world for the histrionic partner and accepting all her drama and unreliability for the sake of the relationship. Unless that's something that sounds appealing to you, steer clear.

PART FOUR

WHAT IS A GOOD PARTNER?

Before we set out to find a great partner, it would be wise to understand what a good partner is. When we start out in life we have only those fairy tales and family templates to guide us, and often it takes years to see past the superficial to what really matters.

> To fall in love is easy, even to remain in it is not difficult; our human loneliness is cause enough. But it is a hard quest worth making to find a comrade through whose steady presence one becomes steadily the person one desires to be. —Anna Louise Strong

Chapter Sixteen

The Secure Base for Life

> In 1970 [early attachment researcher John] Bowlby gave a lecture on "Self-reliance and Some Conditions That Promote It," which made it plain that he saw secure attachment in adulthood affecting not only the quality of one's parenting but the quality of one's entire emotional life. "Evidence is accumulating," he said, "that human beings of all ages are happiest and able to deploy their talents to best advantage when they are confident that, standing behind them there are one or more trusted persons who will come to their aid should difficulties arise." He called the trusted person an attachment figure and, borrowing from Ainsworth, said that such a figure offered the companion a secure base. He believed that the ties to the parent gradually weaken as the child gets older and that the secure base function is slowly shifted to other figures, eventually resting fully on one's mate.[55]

The *secure base* is the foundation of attachment security; in childhood this is created for the child by parental responsiveness. In adulthood, the "others" one can rely on become trusted friends, co-workers, and most importantly, spouses. We all know people who are unable to be alone for long before getting restless and needing some company;

Bowlby also thought the ability to be quietly absorbed in a task or creatively use alone-ness was another benefit of having a secure base:

> Although Bowlby rarely spoke of solitude, of the importance of being able to be happily alone, of the creativity and self-knowledge that can come in times of stillness, he did believe that (like self-reliance) the capacity for healthy solitude in adult life arises from being secure in the realm of attachment and having a secure base to return to.[56]

A good partner assists you by providing that secure base, which in turns allows you to face with honesty and emotional security the difficulties of life and the hard work required to reach your goals. Ideally a partner understands your goals, helps you reach them when you really need it, and is self-sufficient enough to not demand attention or assistance when not truly necessary. The ideal partner communicates with honesty and tact, telling you everything you need to know about how he or she feels and encouraging you to be honest by accepting your communicated feelings even when it is hard. Marriage (or any long-term relationship) takes work and the humility to recognize your own faults and weaknesses, while valuing your partner's needs and goals. It means valuing your partnership beyond your day-to-day desires and petty needs.

> No relationship is perfect, ever. There are always some ways you have to bend, to compromise, to give something up in order to gain something greater… The love we have for each other is bigger than these small differences. And

that's the key. It's like a big pie chart, and the love in a relationship has to be the biggest piece. Love can make up for a lot. —Sarah Dessen

A good partner is reliable and available to help on call, whenever possible; a good partner leaves his partner alone when help is not needed, staying quietly available behind the scenes—nothing is more dispiriting than a bossy partner who horns in on a project and takes it over, which sends the message that he believes his partner is incapable and incompetent. On the other hand, being available to lend a hand and quietly correct errors before they happen is the essence of good caregiving; the company in the task and the intuition of the need for help mirror the best parenting practice. The message is that you are there and you support their goals for growth.

The *New York Times* has an excellent story on the stress reduction and health and immune system benefits of a happy marriage; in one study, when they were holding their partner's hand, the happily married were able to sustain painful shocks with far lower brain activity associated with pain:

> [Professor] Coan says the study simulates how a supportive marriage and partnership gives the brain the opportunity to outsource some of its most difficult neural work. "When someone holds your hand in a study or just shows that they are there for you by giving you a back rub, when you're in their presence, that becomes a cue that you don't have to regulate your negative emotion," he told me. "The other person is essentially regulating your negative

emotion but without your prefrontal cortex. It's much less wear and tear on us if we have someone there to help regulate us."[57]

This positive effect of close companions and spouses has been known since the time of the Greeks. In the *Odyssey*, the shipwrecked Odysseus, trying to return to his homeland and wife after the Trojan War, meets Nausicaä the princess and asks for her help:

> Only yesterday, the twentieth day, did I escape the wine dark sea. Till then the waves and the rushing gales had swept me on from the island of Ogygia. Now some power has tossed me here, doubtless to suffer still more torments on your shores. I can't believe they'll stop. Long before that the gods will give me more, still more.
>
> Compassion—princess, please! You, after all my suffering, you're the first human face I've seen in years. All my friends have died and my family has forgotten me. I know no one else, none in your city, no one in your land.
>
> Show me the way to town, give me a rag for cover, just some cloth, some wrapper you carried with you here. And may the good gods give you all your heart desires: husband, and house, and lasting harmony too.
>
> No finer, greater gift in the world than that... when man and woman possess their home, two minds, two hearts that work as one. Despair to their enemies, joy to all their friends. Their own best claim to glory.

There is much controversy about self-esteem in our culture,

and efforts to build it. Does a good partner take your side no matter what? If self-esteem is based on *real* achievements, *realistic* self-evaluation including both strengths and weaknesses, and a secure base of self-worth built by responsive caregivers in childhood, it is a marvelous and healthy thing, allowing a person to undertake difficult but possible tasks with confidence.

As we have seen with the dismissive-avoidant and the narcissist, it is common that apparent high self-esteem is actually harmful when it is a defense mechanism, not built on real achievements but used as a shield against a sense of worthlessness left by a lack of responsive caregiving in childhood. The "self-esteem movement," which suggested every child should get a prize and aimed at assuring children they were capable and competent by lowering standards so that no one failed or lost a competition, is now seen as a mistake, creating false self-esteem that crumbled immediately when children grew up to discover that reality did not confer awards to every competitor. In the long run, a healthy self-image is realistic—and it does not help if praise or criticism is so obviously unrealistic that the receiver loses confidence in the giver, or worse takes the false as true and makes mistakes in judgment based on the false information. A partner's goal should be to provide *realistic* support that helps his partner achieve the goals that will give them true self-esteem.

So if one's partner or friend has entered a competition of some sort, it is helpful to say, "I hope you win!", or "You've improved a lot at [activity], now you get to compete!"—it is not helpful to say (unless it's true), "You're the best, I know it!", or "You're going to win!" It is always okay to say, "I love you and I'll be there to cheer you on!" The correct message is that *you support their efforts to make their way in the real world with realistic expectations, and that the goal is to work toward improvement together, not perfection.* Constructive criticism accompanied by a message of love and support for mutual goals is always in order.

CHAPTER SEVENTEEN

CULTURAL EVOLUTION OF PAIR BONDS

The earliest human beings had fully developed attachment systems and appear to have pair-bonded, as did some of the hominids before them. Our long evolution through the Stone Age as hunter-gatherers, then in settled agricultural villages and then cities, reinforced and multiplied the survival value of human bonding. Many cultures featured polygamy, which allowed wealthier men to have several wives—the "alpha male" syndrome, as in other hominid societies, giving more powerful men greater sexual and reproductive access. There was little thought of romance or marrying for love; affection between partners was thought of as a nice bonus when it occurred, but marriages were primarily functional and allowed distribution of labor, childrearing, and clarification of inheritance. You didn't marry your partner so much as marry into his family (in most cultures but not all, the bride physically left her family and became a member of the husband's family.) What we now think of as traditional—a romantic and sexually exclusive union between one man and one woman—has only been common around the world in the last two centuries, but the idea of marrying for love is sweeping the rest of the world today as another Western cultural import, carried in movies, music, and stories.

As material progress occurred and elements of society climbed Maslow's Pyramid of Needs to the higher elevations of self-actualization, the fulfillment of the basic need for love began to be seen as a more important part of the pair-bonding contract. An ideal marriage came to be seen not only as a contract for the preservation of wealth and power for the family and promotion of future children, but as a source of companionship and happiness for the partners. In Europe, the Renaissance and Enlightenment of the 16th-18th centuries allowed wealthy urban gentry to *pursue happiness* as a respectable ideal, and the Industrial Revolution that followed created such material abundance that a large middle class was also free to consider partners not selected by their parents, and chosen for mutual happiness.

The customs we now think of as traditional, therefore, are not very old at all; and the enormous increase in life expectancies at puberty (from 30 additional years in preindustrial times to 70 today) has expanded the amount of time we might be together with a partner. In the 18th century agricultural villages most of our ancestors lived in, one might marry at 18, have many children quickly (half of them to die in childhood), be old and tired at 45, and dead by 60. Today we have a much longer span of life with much more wealth and leisure, and that leaves us with a set of evolved customs that don't necessarily fit the new environment. You now get more than one chance to find the right partner for you, without the social disapproval divorce used to carry. So in this new environment, no one should be surprised that more marriages end in divorce—divorce is a luxury we, with our increased career opportunities for women and material abundance, can now afford when a marriage is not working.

Another sign of progress: as marriage has become a contract between partners for happiness as much as property or children, many jurisdictions now recognize marriage between same-sex partners, equally motivated by love.

CHAPTER EIGHTEEN

THE TYRANNY OF THE FAIRY TALE

So "romance," as a factor in seeking out a life partner, can be seen as a luxury good. The ideal for the upper classes is often said to have been developed by medieval troubadours singing of courtly love. The code of chivalry allowed the pure and chaste love of a knight for his lady, which was seen as pure because it was nonsexual—and thus the shocking nature of the adulterous affair between Sir Lancelot and Guinevere, wife of King Arthur in the legend. As we saw in the speech by Odysseus to Nausicaä a few pages back, the concept of partners as two different-but-equals back-to-back facing the world existed even in Homer's day. This may not have been the mushy kind of courtly love promoted in the Middle Ages, but it is fairly close to the modern sensibility of a happy marriage. Of course Odysseus was a king, and commoners may not have had time for such thoughts.

But the ideals of romance remain culturally strong; every fairy tale, every Disney animation, (almost) every Hollywood and Bollywood movie idealize the One True Love, who you will see across a crowded room at just the right moment, fall madly in love with, marry, and live happily ever after with in a vine-covered cottage with a picket fence.

The hazard of such modern cultural programming:

> One day we realize that we are completely possessed and dominated by a set of beliefs that we, as individuals, never chose. It is as though we breathe them in from novels and movies, from the psychological air around us, and they become part of us, as though fused with the cells of our bodies. We all know that we are supposed to "fall in love" and that our relationships must be based on romance—nothing less will do! Every man knows what he is entitled to demand from his [partner.] It is spelled out in detail in some unseen layer of the unconscious mind. This is "romance". —anonymous

Note the word "demand." It is a self-centered expectation that *my* needs will be satisfied, *my* happiness will come from *my* partner. This is a child's narcissistic view of a relationship—it's all about *me*. The fairy tale model tells you you are *entitled* to happiness and your partner is to provide it. Or else! Of course this is not a relationship of adult equals in loving attachment—it has no place for real life, for struggle toward goals, for temporary unhappiness and loss for the sake of a future goal. And those who cling to it generally fail.

Idealized romantic love was not considered especially desirable before Medieval troubadours promoted it. Adult long-term relationships have historically been about family, property, and influence, with eventual love a desirable but not necessary factor. In wealthy urban societies, long-term married persons often sought sexual outlets and the thrills of romance from secondary relationships.

Having as a goal a romantic, *monogamous* partnership is a good strategy only if you are the kind of person who can be happy living in such a relationship. Expecting one's basic nature to be tamed by commitment to such a relationship is not wise—chances are good you will find reasons to uncommit, to cheat, and to ultimately project onto your partner the negative feelings that arise from dishonesty and denying your own nature. Duplicity breeds compartmentalization—dishonesty with your partner becomes rationalization and dishonesty with yourself. Illicit sex outside of your most important relationship can carry risk of disease, and if you have young children who find out about it, can damage their sense of family security. Be honest with yourself about this, and be honest with your partner—many a strong and happy marriage can survive affairs and mistresses, but rarely does one survive dishonesty and carelessness.

In the *New York Times* article "Married, With Infidelities,"[58] writer Mark Oppenheimer discusses the ups and downs of monogamy in an increasingly unmonogamous world, with the typical couple less and less likely to have children in the home and politicians daily caught *in flagrante*. Navigating this new world if you commit to monogamy and are still limerent and untempted, or have children in the home, is a bit easier because of those reinforcing factors; what's harder is what happens later when your partner seems unsexy and you are tempted by others. The business trip, the hotel bar, the admirer you're almost surprised to discover you still can attract… these can be off ramps to disaster if you are not careful and thoroughly honest about what you are doing.

What is *fidelity?* One dictionary says, "Faithfulness to a person, cause, or belief, demonstrated by continuing loyalty and support." The English idiom "true to" captures what this means: true to the commitment made, having faith and trust in the other. This means being always conscious of what your partner feels, and acting to ensure they not only are not hurt but benefit from your words and deeds. Truthfulness about what you think and feel is the foundation. One partner's sex with someone else can seem threatening to the other partner, but like any other action with emotional risks, letting your partner into your thoughts to understand why you might want such a thing makes it something you can talk about together, and perhaps allow. This choice is not for everyone, but the extreme cases (when one partner is disabled and unable to have sex, for example) are easy to understand.

Many people—straight and gay men and women—still believe the Fairy Tale of how unions form and stay together. The Fairy Tale is that "We're in love, he would never hurt me, she will never get sick, we will own a home and two cars and we'll always have enough money and be safe and the sex will be really great and we'll never have a gloomy day."

This list of Fairy Tale assumptions contributed by a friend is amusing:

> *There is only one person for me.* Really? With five billion other people walking around, that's a rather unlikely assumption. If you can only partner with one person on the planet, it seems more likely your requirements are so

demanding there is no one who could meet them. It's probably wiser to strive to be the kind of person who could be a good partner to lots of people. Yes, they should be very special—but not the only one!

Money doesn't matter. Only when you're rich. You have to be able to talk about money. Who makes what? Does the person who brings in more money have a bigger say in how it gets spent? Do you have a spending plan? A savings plan? What if one of you gets a great job opportunity in another city—will you move?

Love will keep us together. Love is not a force in the world. It doesn't pay the bills or get you a job or make you smart; in fact, you could argue the reverse. Love is a reason to try hard, to go above and beyond, and to accomplish things that ordinarily you wouldn't do. Because no one is perfect and even your perfect life-partner will forget to take out the garbage or will wake you up with his incessant snoring.

You can only love one person at a time. Attraction is a function of brain chemistry. Companionate love is what remains when the limerence finally leaves. There's nothing to prevent you from having strong feelings for more than one person. You have an infinite capacity to love.

This relationship will never end. All relationships end. Everyone dies. Everyone's circumstances change. Instead of imbuing one relationship with magic picked up in an after-school special, it might be worthwhile to tell someone how much they mean to you and then work on showing that. Because words are cheap. Signing on a dotted line for a mortgage or having children or jointly caring for family elders shows that you're not just another bed warmer. And all those people in high school you absolutely loved? You won't even remember their names in 30 years.

People should love me for who I am. Oh dear. Have some more kool-aid. Just because you exist doesn't make you lovable. If you have to do things to manipulate how people feel about you, then you are a mess. Clean your mess and stop using other people until you have.

Sex is bad. Don't buy into that. Sex is neither good nor bad. It is a natural function, like eating and breathing. Using sex as a weapon for nonconsensual dominance or withholding sex as punishment are childish games.

I am the center of the world. You may be pretty and smart, but there are many people who are prettier and smarter and they do more chores and make more money and can run marathons. Just be your best. Love your friends. Talk to your kids. Do a good job.

The world owes me. The world doesn't give a rat's ass about you, nor should it. You are no more important (and no less important) than anyone else.

People never change. Do you think your mother married a balding oaf whose idea of a good time is to fart the alphabet? Did your father marry a woman because of her intense bingo addiction and her desire to wear polyester stretch pants in colors not found in nature?

My sweetheart will love me if we have children. It is morally wrong to use other people, especially children, to get what you want. Having babies to keep your man in a marriage does not work. Leaving your wife and kids because you don't like children makes you a douche, not a dad.

I can change him or her. Guess what? Alcoholism, obesity, compulsive gambling, drug addiction, and sex addiction don't exist because of you. You can't fix them. You can help them get help but you have to understand that you are not the change agent.

You have to be honest about what you want and how you feel. You have to give honest feedback. Lying helps no one.[59]

Chapter Nineteen

More About Codependence

Earlier, *codependence* was discussed and dismissed as an overused term implying that normal partner interdependence was somehow dysfunctional.

The concept and terminology came out of the Alcoholics Anonymous movement; the addicted were seen as trapped in a web of dependency with others (their *enablers,* or codependents) who made excuses for and assisted the addicts in avoiding the consequences of their addiction, making their impaired life seem more normal and postponing the ultimate reckoning that would force the addicts to change their lives.

Pop psychologists and media spread this idea far and wide, and today almost any relationship can be tagged "codependent," as if the unitary self-sufficiency of the dismissive was the ideal state and any reliance on others weak and unhealthy. Of course a close relationship has features of mutual dependency! So when do we begin to call interdependence dysfunctional? One key may be purpose: is the interdependence advancing the capabilities of both of the partners, or is it creating a stagnant holding pattern that is preventing further growth? The highest interdependence of all occurs between parents and child; but this is a temporary state where effective parenting is creating an independent adult who will ideally function well in the world. Spouses and close friends may pine for each other when apart, yet their mutual emotional support allows them to achieve and further their own development.

It certainly happens that feelings of attachment between, for example, a narcissist and his current enabler create a dysfunctional holding pattern keeping reality from harming the narcissist's fragile self-regard. This also happens when an alcoholic is shielded by her husband from the consequences of her addiction until it is too late. Hoping against all reasonable hope that the pattern will change and trying to pretend that you can keep harm from your loved one by covering up problems and placing their short-term feelings above what would actually be best for them, and yourself, is a mistake we can all understand and sympathize with. That is what dysfunctional codependence looks like.

Avoidants, particularly the dismissive-avoidant, flee to their Fortress of Solitude when intimacy turns threatening, and it is with them that the fad for declaring relationships codependent causes the most trouble. It is not unusual for a Dismissive to explain to his current romantic partner that he finds her desire for responses and attention to be "codependent." It's an all-purpose rationalization suggesting that partners owe each other only what limited attention and care they can spare from their busy lifestyles.

The "just when needed, just the right amount" principle of

responsiveness is ideal between the best partners, and best friends. For the avoidant types, a willingness to tolerate some dependence on significant others is a sign of improvement; and for the severely anxious-preoccupied, being able to leave their partner be when he's busy without starting to worry is a sign of growing security.

CHAPTER TWENTY

LIMERENCE VS. LOVE

> Limerence is an involuntary state of mind which results from a romantic attraction to another person combined with an overwhelming, obsessive need to have one's feelings reciprocated. Psychologist Dorothy Tennov [60] coined the term "limerence" in her 1979 book *Love and Limerence: The Experience of Being in Love* [61] to describe the concept that had grown out of her work in the mid-1960s, when she interviewed over 500 people on the topic of love. [62]

Being "in love"—*limerence*—is involuntary; you have no conscious control over the creeping obsession and the hormonal-biochemical imperative to Pay Attention to this Fascinating New Creature in your world. One common explanation for limerence is that it serves the evolutionary purpose by irrationally binding couples long enough to rear children. Some recent reading suggests a higher-level game-theoretic signalling purpose: to demonstrate that one's commitment to the other is irrational and therefore unlikely to be broken by the attraction of a more suitable and advantageous partner. Someone considering a partner can be convinced to commit more easily when evidence shows the partner will not break the commitment just because a better opportunity comes along. The persuasive power of a display of unconditional and irrational love is enormous.[63]

Culturally, limerence is either seen as the desirable state of hyperexcitement all romances should begin with, or the tragic downfall of clueless losers who throw themselves at people they barely know because of some delusional intuition that they must be soulmates. Both of these views are oversimplified—many or even most good long-term relationships start off with a long, slow period of getting-to-know-you, gradually easing into partnership. The limerence that may be present in one (and occasionally both!) prospective partners can help get over the initial hurdle of superficial difficulties in getting them together. Being "in love" is not a necessary or sufficient condition for partnering with someone, but neither does it hurt.

But our culture glorifies drama and passion. Novels, opera, movies all tell us sexual attraction plus passion equals Really Living. Dr. Lewis has some thoughtful comments:

> Our society goes the craziness of in love one better by insisting on the supremacy of delectable but ephemeral madness. Cultural messages inform the populace that if they aren't perpetually electric they are missing out on the pinnacle of relatedness. Every pop-cultural medium portrays the height of adult intimacy as the moment when two attractive people who don't know a thing about each other tumble into bed and have passionate sex. All the waking moments of our love lives should tend, we are told, toward that throbbing, amorous apotheosis. But in love merely brings the players together, and the end of that

prelude is as inevitable as it is desirable. True relatedness has a chance to blossom only with the waning of its intoxicating predecessor.

Loving is limbically distinct from in love. Loving is mutuality; loving is synchronous attunement and modulation. As such, adult love depends critically upon knowing the other. In love demands only the brief acquaintance necessary to establish an emotional genre but does not demand that the book of the beloved's soul be perused from preface to epilogue. Loving derives from intimacy, the prolonged and detailed surveillance of a foreign soul.[64]

The rush of initial limerence is so powerful it is analogous to a psychoactive drug—indeed, some of the same neurotransmitter receptors may be involved. And by analogy, we have Roxy Music's "Love is the Drug."[65] A self-help book, Peele and Brodsky's *Love and Addiction*[66], covers the topic of people addicted to the rush and unable to stop craving it. Stalkers are people who have fallen into a pathologically deep limerent hole, unable to overcome the delusion that they have a special relationship with the stalked.

But long-term relationships are built on a much deeper jointly-built understanding, and a more durable limbic connection between partners. This requires regular physical contact, a long history of supportive message exchange, and a deep sense of trust and knowledge of the other:

Because loving is reciprocal physiologic influence, it entails a deeper and more literal connection than most realize. Limbic regulation affords lovers the ability to modulate each other's emotions, neurophysiology, hormonal status, immune function, sleep rhythms, and stability. If one leaves on a trip, the other may suffer insomnia, a delayed menstrual cycle, a cold that would have been fought off in the fortified state of togetherness. The neurally ingrained Attractors of one lover warp the emotional virtuality of the other, shifting emotional perceptions— what he feels, sees, knows. When somebody loses his partner and says a part of him is gone, he is more right than he thinks. A portion of his neural activity depends on the presence of that other living brain. Without it, the electric interplay that makes up him has changed. Lovers hold keys to each other's identities, and they write neurostructural alterations into each other's networks. Their limbic tie allows each to influence who the other is and becomes.

Mutuality has tumbled into undeserved obscurity by the primacy our society places on the art of the deal. The prevailing myth reaching most contemporary ears is this: relationships are 50-50. When one person does a nice thing for the other, he is entitled to an equally pleasing benefit—the sooner the better, under the terms of this erroneous dictum. The physiology of love is no barter. Love is simultaneous mutual regulation, wherein each person meets the needs of the other, because neither can provide for his own. Such a relationship is not 50-50—it's 100-100. Each takes perpetual care of the other, and, within concurrent reciprocity, both thrive. For those who attain it, the benefits of deep attachment are powerful— regulated people feel whole, centered, alive. With their physiology stabilized from the proper source, they are resilient to the stresses of daily life, or even to those of extraordinary circumstance.[67]

Being "in love" is the Fool's Gold of attachment: non-nourishing, short-lived, and more a hindrance to long-term achievement than a help.

Chapter Twenty-One

What About Sex?

Good sex is like glue—it helps hold together a good relationship, and it's one of the most important ways to bond partners. This does not mean a sexless relationship will not last—studies show up to 20% of long-term relationships have little or no sexual component, often because over time one or both partners have lost interest. This does not mean the relationship should end, since there are many other important reasons why a long-term relationship continues, but it does make the relationship more likely to be seen as unhappy or unfulfilling.

If you're young you are probably wondering, how that is even possible! Together without sex? Well, as you get older you'll come to understand that you don't live in the best of all possible worlds, where everyone is healthy, hormones are surging, and sexual libido is something you struggle to restrain. As time goes by, partners age, concerns of childrearing and career cause stress and take up time, and the habit of having sex can be lost in the shuffle. Interest in sex varies, and some people are basically uninterested in it—yet those people usually find partners. The common perception (among the young) that hot sex must be at the heart of all happy marriages is simply wrong.

That said, if you are young and looking for your first partner, you almost certainly put sexual attractiveness near the top of your list of desirable characteristics in a partner. Sex is important, and especially in the first few years, can make up for a lot of practical issues that come up; makeup sex after a fight notoriously reminds partners of a really good reason to put up with each other's foibles.

While sex is important, you should also be aware in the back of your mind that sexual attractiveness naturally fades with time. While some couples have satisfying sex into their 80s, the most important factors in keeping you together are not sexual, but companionate—does your partner make you laugh? Can you count on him when you need him? Does he understand and sympathize with your feelings? Can you support each other in getting things done? If your relationship is primarily founded on sex, then little will hold you together should that fade, and it most likely will (the "seven-year itch"[68] being a shorthand term for the phenomenon of dissatisfaction with a relationship once the limerence has faded and the sex grown routine). And then the world will seem to be full of people both of you find more sexually compelling even if just for sheer novelty—if you are not loyal to each other because of a deep attachment bond based on trust and history, then such attractions will tear your relationship apart. Be wary of committing to a partner who offers great sex but seemingly not much more.

PART FIVE

THE SEARCH FOR A GOOD PARTNER

In this part we'll talk about how you should go about looking for a good partner, informed by what you have learned about attachment types.

Chapter Twenty-Two

The Search

Since time's beginning, romantic partners have searched for each other with exquisite but obscure deliberation. "In literature, as in love," wrote Andre Maurois, "we are astonished at what is chosen by others." And they are every bit as amazed at us. The very concept of "compatibility" discloses that no all-purpose template for loving predominates. Sexual attractiveness contributes only a minor filter to this selectivity. The number of couples who marry is a minuscule fraction of the many who find each other physically interesting. Not just anyone will do; in fact, to any one person looking for a mate, almost nobody will. A lover tests the combination of himself plus serial others like a child juxtaposing jigsaw pieces until a pair snaps home. Love's puzzle work is done in the dark: prospective partners hunt blindly; they cannot describe the person they seek. Most do not even realize, as they grope for the geographical outline of a potential piece, that their own heart is a similar marvel of specificity. How do these delicately shaped desires develop? By what means do people learn the discriminating taste that tells them how and whom to love? And why does that knowledge remain opaque to their mind's eye?[69]

Common advice in dating is to stick with people you meet

through community: church, work, school, or friends-of-friends. While there are significant advantages in this advice —it's an excellent way to screen out the dangerous or irresponsible, since your community will likely warn you of any bad reputation or previous poor behavior of this person —you may not be so lucky as to have a large group of suitable candidates in your community. Cities have their singles bars, although these have become less important as the Internet has brought online dating and hookup applications. If you are looking for a partner, a service like eHarmony now helps screen candidates by attachment type as well as other compatibility factors, which can save a lot of time kissing frogs. But always meet anyone you have contacted online in a public place, and look for connections—does he or she know anyone you know, work in a place you know, live in a neighborhood near enough to you to be practical for dating? Until you have some verified information on this person's background, beware of getting in too deep or spending time alone with him or her.

CHAPTER TWENTY-THREE

DATING, BY AGE

Some things about dating never change. But there are some differences that arise as you and your cohort mature that vary by age group.

High School

Welcome, young person! If you are reading this book, you're rather advanced for your age. It's certainly possible to find and bond to a long-term partner at this age, but it is uncommon for such an early relationship to end up being your lifelong choice. Most relationships you are likely to have are going to be training relationships—you will fall in with someone you find superficially interesting and fun, but in most cases it won't work out, either because one or both of you are still too self-centered and short-term-oriented to sacrifice for the sake of the relationship, or because circumstances (college or parental objections) come between you. This is best seen as a time to practice and learn about other people and yourself, to try out different ways of acting and feeling to see how they fit you. And when it does happen you are both mature enough and compatible enough to form a permanent bond, go for it—you will both know if that's really the case. And if it doesn't work out, you have a lot of life ahead of you to do better.

20s

Prime time to meet and start a family, if that's what you want. In recent years, young people have waited longer and longer to get together as education and career have taken longer to get settled; many grad students and professionals wait until their late 20s now. This is probably the best age to quickly meet an appropriate partner, since most people are still single and the "good ones" haven't settled into their happy and long-lasting relationships yet. Round 1 of the marriage game is the easiest one to win, if you yourself are secure and mature enough. If you are more anxious or insecure, or have yet to fully mature in all the other areas of life, you will often make a mistake in this round and end up with Mr. or Ms. Wrong. But only experience can teach you, if you weren't lucky enough to have the kind of healthy family support that makes you a great partner from Day One.

One of the obvious issues in this age group is a fixation on the superficial and the short-term. In big cities fleets of singles mingle in clubs and bars; the art of the pickup is still on full display. You might meet just the right person in a bar after a few hours of talk, but most likely not. Still, hanging out with friends and meeting their friends is one of the classic ways to find someone, so anywhere they are, you might find someone just right. And it's good practice.

In this age group most people are looking for their first

serious relationship. One common error is latching onto the first person you meet who actually wants you (you!)—seeing this first romantic interest so over-optimistically (because you are so grateful to be wanted!) that you forget to take the time to really get to know them before committing. The selfish "fairy tale" ideal will still be in full force for most of you, especially women—many women have been trained by their family to see themselves as little princesses to be served and pampered, which is a huge problem in dealing with real life. Meanwhile, young men are just getting their bearings and not all will be confident enough to appear good partner material to a young woman (or man, as the case may be.) Overcoming insecurities and succeeding professionally is this age group's goal.

30s

You and yours probably have at least one relationship behind you now, and you vow not to make that mistake again. But there are so many ways to make a mistake! The dating pool is less attractive and carries a bit more baggage—kids, bankruptcies, harridan exes, and percentage-wise the seemingly available men are starting to be predominately dismissive. Your friends are either married or too busy to be hanging out in clubs chatting up strangers, and so are you. Finding good candidates is harder than it was, and more caution is needed since they are more likely to have hidden issues. If you haven't had a good long-term relationship yet, especially if you have rotated through girl or boyfriends monthly or yearly for several years, you should ask yourself if you are the problem—by this point most people who fit that pattern are demonstrating that they simply aren't able to keep a good relationship going. Do you think all of your exes are crazy? Have many of them told you you were just not there for them? Look to yourself and fix your issues before hurting yet another person.

After 40

So you're older now, and you think wiser. But still embedded in your thought processes are all of those myths about romance and the ideal partner just waiting for you out there like some used, rusty needle in a mildewed haystack.

Viewed dispassionately, what are the odds that all of these things will happen: a) you find a person that elicits a really strong emotional response; and b) they feel the same about you; and c) they are capable of being an ideal partner to you (single, interesting for years, matching in values, makes you laugh...), and vice-versa? The odds are pretty slim, in middle age, when most of the interesting candidates are already taken. So maybe you should think about whether each of those conditions is necessary....

The kind of bond that holds most really long-term relations together is not the intense, dramatic love you've been told all your life is a necessary precondition. It's more a feeling that only grows in time, and has to do with mutual reliance, trust, respect, and a more mild affection. It's not clear that there's any correlation between the people who spark a more intense initial limerence in you and the desired person who would make you happy in the long run. Immediate passion and stunning looks rarely lead people to the right person for the long term; look for the best *partner,* and be happy. You should seriously question your assumption that if you're not feeling *in love* after a few months, it's no good; and you might be careful to find partner candidates who are patient and have evolved beyond a need to have the intense romance they have been told all their lives they are due. Pay more attention to the boredom signal: "I am with X and I'd rather be somewhere else, with someone else, who's *interesting.*" That's deadly in the long run.

So when you're dating someone, ignore your checklist of requirements and pay attention to your feelings. Do you enjoy being with him or her? Does it feel like you can count on your maybe-future-partner? Everything else is noise.

CHAPTER TWENTY-FOUR

WHAT TYPE IS COMPATIBLE?

If you're a **secure** type yourself, you have a wide choice of partners—other Secures, or with more effort and drama, you can patiently work with the anxious-preoccupied and avoidant. But if you are attracted to a certain non-secure person and love them enough to help them achieve some attachment security, you should know that you are going to have to be the secure base for both of you—it is your firm foundation and good sense of self that will anchor both of you, and bring your partner toward a security that will allow them to calmly come to your aid when you need it. It is not hopeless, but it is a challenge that most of us would not choose if we had realized going in how much effort and time would be required, and if you are a young person trying to build a career, you will not be getting the calm support you could use to allow you to focus on your work. This is why Secures who succeed in this anchoring process are called saints.

Anxious-preoccupied types do poorly with each other—two needy, clingy people who do manage to calm each other's insecurities exist as couples, but it's rare, and the resulting relationship is closer to unhealthy codependence; neither will be strengthened by the bond. A mildly Preoccupied person can last with a mildly Avoidant sort, but the relationship tends to be unhappy as the bond is based on the unmet neediness of the Preoccupied and the willingness of the Avoidant to accept the attention without providing emotional security. A preoccupied person is much better off with a Secure who can gradually calm the preoccupied person's insecurities by steady love and support, as in this case:

> The preoccupied wife who had ambivalent attachment to her parent cannot believe her husband when he says, despite their fights and mutual dissatisfactions, that he genuinely loves her and wants to stay with her. She cannot assimilate it to her worldview, her internal model. She is sure he will abandon her, either because he already wants to or because her impossible and anxious neediness will eventually drive him out. But his steadfastness over the years builds her trust. It causes her to remember her relationship with a great uncle, whose love was precious and unwavering, and to think more and more about him and how good she felt about herself around him. Gradually, she assimilates her marriage to this model, and it becomes more central. Feeling more secure, she now finds herself freer to reflect on the past.[70]

Though is appears a preoccupied person might be better off with a secure partner, some research indicates that in this case opposites attract:

> A number of studies have looked into the question of whether we are attracted to people based on their attachment style or ours. Two researchers in the field of adult attachment, Paula Pietromonaco, of the University of

Massachusetts, and Katherine Carnelley, of the University of Southampton in the UK, found that avoidant individuals actually prefer anxiously attached people. Another study, by Jeffry Simpson of the University of Minnesota, showed that anxious women are more likely to date avoidant men. Is it possible, then, that people who guard their independence with ferocity would seek the partners most likely to impinge on their autonomy? Or that people who seek closeness are attracted to people who want to push them away? And if so, why? Pietromonaco and Carnelley believe that these attachment styles actually complement each other in a way. Each reaffirms the other's beliefs about themselves and about relationships. The avoidants' defensive self-perception that they are strong and independent is confirmed, as is the belief that others want to pull them into more closeness than they are comfortable with. The anxious types find that their perception of wanting more intimacy than their partner can provide is confirmed, as is their anticipation of ultimately being let down by significant others. So, in a way, each style is drawn to reenact a familiar script over and over again.[71]

This kind of complementary dysfunction can lead to a stable relationship, but one where both partners stay in their insecure styles, with the preoccupied battling for every scrap of attention and the avoidant one only giving enough to confirm his view of attachment as a necessary evil. These attractions are based on re-enacting the dysfunctional touch and response cycles of their early childhoods, and generally these couples report they are together despite their unhappiness.

Levine and Heller point out that the slights and intermittent reinforcement of the attractive avoidant male often trigger activation of the attachment system—producing intrigue and sparks. So what if he only answers your text messages days later, if at all? He's hot and just hard-to-get enough that you really want him! This is the terrible mistake so many make: they meet a secure guy and it's all so drama-free that they think he's dull:

> If you are anxious, the reverse of what happens when you meet someone avoidant happens when you meet someone secure. The messages that come across from someone secure are very honest, straightforward, and consistent. Secures are not afraid of intimacy and know they are worthy of love. They don't have to beat around the bush or play hard to get. Ambiguous messages are out of the mix, as are tension and suspense. As a result, your attachment system remains relatively calm. Because you are used to equating an activated attachment system with love, you conclude that this can't be "the one" because no bells are going off. You associate a calm attachment system with boredom and indifference. Because of this fallacy you might let the perfect partner pass you by.[72]

So armed with foreknowledge, a wise preoccupied person will seek out a Secure and avoid the sometimes attractive but ultimately unsupportive Avoidant of both flavors, as well as other Preoccupieds, who are likely to be the worst partners of all for them.

The **avoidant** types are the least likely to form a positive attachment bond with their partners, and the Dismissive flavor especially tend to be single or rapidly go through partners, since their psyche refuses to recognize any dependency on the bond and suppresses any feelings of love and attachment. Both types are almost never found coupled with another avoidant person, since in such a relationship there is no one to start the signaling cycle that keeps a relationship going. At least **fearful-avoidant** types are aware that they need attachment and are more likely to be reachable by a secure or preoccupied person, but with the unfortunate tendency to end relationships because they subconsciously fear rejection and would rather reject first; and they also have the general avoidant tendency to not feel love or other attachment emotions very consciously.

To be realistic, if you are severely **avoidant,** your best hope of a happy long-term relationship is with a secure person who is willing to wait patiently and work with you on your inability to feel or express your feelings, and who understands your fear of being truly close to anyone. If you spend your time pretending to be in relationships with people who inevitably disappoint you, the problem is not them, it's you. If you get involved with a preoccupied person who accepts your mistreatment, you will have a partner but neither of you will be very happy unless you both work hard at making each other feel more secure.

If you are **dismissive-avoidant**, it must have been an unusual chain of events that led you to read this book, because in general Dismissives have no conscious interest in learning how to make a relationship work, and it would rarely occur to them to try to change themselves to make themselves more loving and sensitive to their partner's inner states. But if you are here, maybe you are willing to undertake the years of therapy and self-examination that might help. We'll get to methods for doing that in a later chapter.

CHAPTER TWENTY-FIVE

TYPES IN THE DATING POOL

Dr. Karen comments "Fonagy found that neither education, intelligence, social or economic status, nor ethnic background have any relationship to this capacity to reflect openly and clearly on the inner state of oneself or others."[73] You may have good reasons for thinking a certain class or occupation or income level partner would be best—and certainly compatibility on these external trappings can ease the way and provide commonality—but there are great relationships that cross all those boundaries, and if you meet someone you click with who happens to be from the other side of the tracks (be the difference racial, cultural, religious, or income class), good partners can climb any mountains between them.

Estimates vary, but a good guess is that 50% of the population starts adulthood secure, while 20% are anxious-preoccupied, 25% are dismissive-avoidant, and 5% are fearful-avoidant. But as time goes by and the secure are more likely to get into and stay in long-term relationships, the proportions of the types seen in the dating pool change—the secure become scarce, and the dismissive-avoidant, who begin and end relationships quickly, become the most likely type you will encounter.

The following graph shows a simulation of the type frequency in the dating population over time given the different expected rates of coupling and breakup for each type:

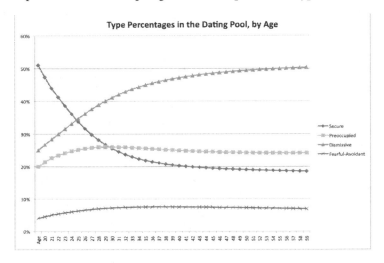

Type Percentages in the Dating Pool, by Age

Graph Showing Types Over Time[74]

This graph is based on a simplified simulation of the dating pool by age, showing the percentage of each type in the shrinking dating pool. Secures appear dominant early in the dating pool at about 50%, but over time their prevalence declines to around 20%. Notice how the Dismissive-Avoidant start off as the second most prevalent attachment type at 25%, but over time become the predominant type at 50% of the far smaller dating population—this is not because they don't start relationships, but that they tend to exit them quickly. The proportion of Preoccupied and Fearful-Avoidant increases somewhat as well. The age scale assumes everyone starts looking for a partner at 20, so subpopulations which start later (academics, for example) would be shifted by a few years. Since both starting parameters and the simulation are simplified, these numbers are only suggestive.

The shrinkage of the dating pool with time and its later domination by less secure types means the older you are, the more cautious you should be, because it is much more likely that those in the dating pool in later years have a problematic attachment type, or even worse problems keeping them from sustaining good relationships. Of course there are always new entries to the dating pool who have been released from good relationships by their partner's death or unfortunate circumstances; but those past 40 who have never been able to get and keep a good relationship going, likely never will—unless of course they have realized they need to change and work hard on themselves.

CHAPTER TWENTY-SIX

DETECTING THE WRONG PEOPLE

So knowing what attachment type you are most likely to do well with, how do you find a partner who matches? Unless you have met your prospective partner through a dating service like eHarmony, which prescreens candidates using simple tests like the one that begins this book, you are faced with the problem of screening out the unlikely partners using red flags and clues they drop during conversation. On a first date you should be looking mostly at nonverbal cues—are you attracted physically, does he or she make you laugh and delight you, is their clumsiness cute or off-putting? But after you have both decided you are at least interested in getting to know each other, *The Conversation*—a wide-ranging revelation of personal and professional history and your feelings—is in order. The first clue that should make you run from a candidate is an inability or unwillingness to describe past attachments (to parents, lovers, and friends) with a frank assessment of feelings at the time; either hiding or being unable to put into words the feelings they have about important others is a sure sign of trouble ahead, be it Dismissive, Anxious, or Narcissistic. No matter how intriguing the mystery may be, do not pursue them; drop them and try someone else before you waste years finding nothing good behind the walls they have put up.

Another red flag in The Conversation is an apparent lack of interest in your story and your feelings. If the conversation always ends up being about him or her and includes long diatribes about past partners or parents without sensing you need a break or letting you talk about similarities to your life, you are talking to an insecure person. No matter how successful or vivacious and attractive this person appears to be, more than likely he or she has few close friends and limited ability to be a good partner to anyone. The dismissive, especially, will often reveal themselves quickly by the extremes of their evaluations of others in their lives—past partners were awful (except possibly one perfect one that got away), while he may say his mother was a saint, and go on and on about the faults of recent past relationships. Run away! Next year he will be just as ungenerous talking about you, if you subject yourself to his mistreatment.

Near the beginning of every relationship, no matter how successful, something will happen that makes you question your partner's suitability—often this will be the shock of their first display of anger toward you or someone else. "Karen" jokes that she almost broke up with the love of her life when they traveled together for the first time and her gung-ho partner tried to get her up to get to a breakfast without giving her time to wash and set her hair, which at the time was an important part of her daily ritual. She was angry that he was so insistent and didn't understand her need to feel good-looking before going out, and he was shocked that the superficially easygoing woman he was dating would snap at him over something so small. If explanations and apologies follow, these are just accidents that happen before you really understand each other's habits and feelings. No real relationship is completely smooth, especially at the beginning. What you look out for is evidence of a lack of consideration for your feelings, or even worse pushing back by claiming you are "too needy" or "clingy."

If your partner-candidate has passed early tests and revealed his or her relationship history in detail—and it seems honest and consistent—you have some data to guess at their attachment type. A man in his 40s with a string of 10-15 apparently crazy ex-girl- or boyfriends is almost certainly the dreaded Avoidant. A woman in her 20s with one or two boyfriends in her past is very possibly Secure, if the discussions of those boyfriends make their breakups sound reasonable. If she has had a series of cold or abusive boyfriends (as she describes them), you are likely with a Preoccupied. If a woman over 40 tells you she had one long and happy relationship, and that relationship ended in death of her partner, you are likely with the rare older Secure person on the dating market. And so on.

If you have been dating someone awhile and you are questioning how their attachment type might be sabotaging the relationship, you can ask them to help you—as good partners willingly do—by completing the questionnaire in this book or the more thorough and easily-scored one online. But if you have been seeing them for awhile, you should recognize by now what type they are after reading the descriptions of the types.

CHAPTER TWENTY-SEVEN

EFFECTIVE DATING

When you are looking and naïve, you will try to make anyone halfway attractive fit your hopes and dreams. It is much better to be less optimistic and employ an attitude of cautious assessment combined with a willingness to move on immediately when the red flag quota has been exceeded—without drama or delay.

Then there is the social requirement (after you're over 25 or so) to have a regular activity partner because everyone else does, which can make you date someone incessantly until it becomes a habit. The insecure are unwilling to let go even though all signs point to a dead-end.

Signals that mislead: one of the most obvious is seeing someone very frequently and exclusively. If that person expects conventional courtship, he will see it as your signal to make a run at coupling up. Not seeing someone as frequently —filling your time by seeing some other people at the same time—and letting it be known that you are staying casual could help brake any such expectation. You are not always available; you are not induced by a need for regular sex or company for going out to give the impression that you are ready for more commitment. Seeing multiple people introduces the health risks of sex with multiple partners, so consider a policy of no sex on at least the first few dates, until you really have found someone you think may be steady date material.

Be aware that there are lots of candidates and if you settle on one exclusively and make them a habit, you are closing yourself to others too soon. You should not date someone exclusively until you are sure they are at least the right attachment type for you. The most common mistake of naïve young people is falling into a relationship with the wrong person and sticking it out for years—or even decades!— because they want to love and nurture their partner. This quality of loyalty should be reserved for someone who can return it. Don't get attached too soon!

If you've spotted red flags, don't tell yourself you're wrong and keep on with this person. Distance them and find others. Because there are better candidates!

If you're anxious-preoccupied, don't settle for an attractive avoidant who keeps you guessing and anxious. Look for a solid, reliable person who will be there for you when you need him. Levine & Heller's *Attached: The New Science of Adult Attachment and How It Can Help You Find—and Keep —Love*[75] has a lot of excellent material on approaching the dating scene when you are anxious-preoccupied—their advice amounts to techniques to keep yourself feeling more secure and approaching the task of dating without getting too caught up in dysfunctional drama.

If you're avoidant, don't pretend to go along with someone's program for you because you like company or need a presentable partner for social occasions. Stay as honest and real about your lack of feelings as you can. This will avoid a lot of pain to others and help you find someone who can tolerate your lack of outward commitment.

If someone treats your feelings as unimportant or lets you down in large or small ways frequently, drop them fast. You are not dreaming, and they will always be that way. Three strikes is enough.

CHAPTER TWENTY-EIGHT

ENDING A PARTNERSHIP

All good things (and bad things) come to an end. Many long-term relationships end, usually because they weren't making one or both partners happy, but often because one or both partners have changed or circumstances force a parting. If both partners recognize the need to move on, the split can be accomplished without damaging either's regard for the other, or ending contact, or requiring mutual friends (or worse, children!) to choose sides. Of course such a constructive ending is more likely when partners have been good communicators all along.

But oftentimes communication has never been good and the relationship was never very happy. Nature's nasty limerence trick, where one is compelled by hormones and desire to mate blindly ("I'm in love!"), can lead to early commitment and starting a family before one or both partners realizes they are making a mistake, and the result can be years of fighting, sorrow, and pain before the marriage is ended.

When our attachment needs aren't being met and we're angry about some failure of our partner to give us support (or, conversely, angry about their unreasonable demands), fighting to hurt can break out. All couples fight, but the danger zone is when one or both no longer respect the other, and treat the other's feelings with contempt. Words can do permanent damage:

> In a way fighting like this was just like using magic. You said the words, and they altered the universe. By merely speaking you could create damage and pain, cause tears to fall, drive people away, make yourself feel better, make your life worse. —Lev Grossman, in The Magicians.[76]

One of the characteristics of those who have a secure attachment style is loyalty. Once chosen, a partner is valued and cared for, *no matter what*—sometimes to the point of staying with a dysfunctional, unequal relationship. This unearned regard for the partner can take years of stress and pain to wear away, leaving a sense of damage and loss. If you find yourself in a bad marriage or partnership, be very honest with yourself—is this going to improve? Does your partner really value you and your feelings as highly as their own? How many years do you want to make excuses for them and rationalize your sticking with them out of misplaced hope and loyalty?

There are good reasons for sticking with a relationship that is not very satisfactory:

- Physical or financial responsibilities
- Dependent children
- Community roles and expectations
- Reasonable hope that both partners will work to improve it

There are really bad reasons, too:
- Belief in the fairy tale
- "I can change him!"
- "It's the best I can do (or hope for, or deserve.)"

No matter when you end a relationship—in your 20s or your 60s—there is someone out there for you who can be a better partner. Strive to be honest and do as little damage as possible if your relationship ends—but get on with finding a better life.

Part Six

Changing Yourself

It can be dismaying to discover that it has been something about you all along that has kept you from finding the right person to settle down with. But everyone who wants a good partner needs to strive to become a good partner themselves; it's only by developing yourself into a person who is rewarding to be with and loyal that you will attract the person that has those qualities for you.

CHAPTER TWENTY-NINE

IF YOU ARE THE PROBLEM

So maybe you recognize yourself as one the the problematic insecure types, or have enough experience with past relationships to recognize that you are fatally attracted to a type that will never be capable of a happy, stable partnership with you. Those would be called *bad attractors*. If you're over 30 years old and you are still caught in the web of your parents' dysfunctions, perhaps it's time to grow up:

> A friend, a woman in her forties, attended a workshop in which she had an important insight on this subject. She had been speaking bitterly of the ways in which her mother had disappointed her since she was a child, when another woman, in her seventies, asked her, "What would you think of me if I attacked my mother at such length?" My friend said, "I guess I would hope that by your age I would have come to terms with all that." The older woman said, "That's exactly what the women here who are in their twenties are thinking about you."[77]

The relationship templates you grew up with can continue to rule your romantic interests even when they are dysfunctional—you learned to be interested and excited by the dramas of your family, and even when they make you unhappy find life without them dull. Perceiving a secure, stable partner as "dull" because they do not operate by creating operatic emotional scenes can cause you to miss some of the best partner candidates you may meet—"He seems kind, but no fireworks! But that bad boy over there, he's hot…"

> The fact that many people find romantic excitement in a lover who displays the qualities of a rejecting parent, an excitement they do not find in others, suggest the degree to which they remain not just committed to but enthralled by early attachment figures, They can't let go of the mother or father who didn't love them the way they needed to be loved. And they continue to be bewitched by the hurtfulness that compromised their care, They are caught in the parental orbit, a hurt child still leaning out for a love that can never be, and blinded to what they are doing by the belief they have no feelings toward their parents at all or have washed their hands of them.[78]

> In intimate relationships… one is fixated on another, more compelling, channel. Here, always playing, is the drama of the rejecting parent and the longing child who is some combination of angry, bad, manipulative, and spurned. Living for this drama, one moves into each relationship playing one or both sides of the pattern. This obsession, this repetitive compulsion, inevitably intensifies one's sense of being bereft of internal goodness, of seeing such goodness as only existing in desperately sought after others, whom one hates and envies as well as loves and desires.[79]

To avoid this kind of cycle which occupies your time and

prevents you from growing beyond bad parental templates, use your logical brain to oversee what your emotional brain is doing. After reading and understanding the emotional signaling system and the attachment types, strive to be more secure yourself and appraise those you meet by those standards to see which are just replaying old games and which are being honest with themselves and others. No one is perfect and everyone has emotional baggage, but look for the ones who can address their problems honestly and work toward a realistic understanding instead of blaming parents and others for their problems.

If you now recognize that you're dismissive or preoccupied, this knowledge alone will help free you from those patterns a bit—as you recognize in your own behaviors the harmful actions (whether distancing or needy) that have driven past friends and partners away, you will be able to intervene to question your own actions. Changing your own attachment style takes time and patience, and is only possible with supportive friends and partners; explaining your inner struggles to them will allow them to see the problem when it happens and help you grow beyond it. There is nothing more valuable in life than a loyal, reliable spouse and friends—live this like you mean it.

If you really want to work on making yourself a better partner, then you can embark on a program of self-improvement. There are self-help books and resources online, and a few therapists who specialize in attachment issues, though most relationship therapists don't directly address those issues.

Chapter Thirty

Self-Help

Self-help books are like car repair manuals: you can read them all day, but doing so doesn't fix a thing. Working on a car means rolling up your sleeves and getting under the hood, and you have to be willing to get dirt on your hands and grease beneath your fingernails. Overhauling emotional knowledge is no spectator sport; it demands the messy experience of yanking and tinkering that comes from a limbic bond. If someone's relationships today bear a troubled imprint, they do so because an influential relationship left its mark on a child's mind. When a limbic connection has established a neural pattern, it takes a limbic connection to revise it.[80]

This sounds discouraging, but if you have understanding friends or a spouse willing to talk about your feelings with you, you can make some progress on your own. Your friends and partners, whether their attachment types are similar to yours or different, will have slightly different histories and perspectives on what is normal in terms of background and upbringing. If you can talk with them honestly about your needs and feelings, they can notice and point out any of your attitudes and expectations that seem odd or unhealthy to them but which you take for granted. You in turn can do the same for them, and that is just another function of personal intimacy. This exchange of views is part of what makes closeness and intimacy so valuable for personal growth, emotional health, and self-actualization.   It's also a major factor in group therapy, as well as specialized support groups (for issues like grief, cancer, amputees, stroke survivors, etc.), since people dealing with similar problems can be examples to others, with helpful advice, encouragement, sympathy, and understanding.

Here are some resources to help you work on your own attachment style issues:

Overview

Lewis, Thomas; Amini, Fari; and Lannon, Richard. *A General Theory of Love*. New York: Vintage Books, 2001. This book is a groundbreaking synthesis of recent scientific work in the study of attachment. It is emotionally moving and accessible, and brings together topics of neuroscience and psychology with a literary sensibility. Should be required reading in college psychology courses.

Karen, Robert. *Becoming Attached: First Relationships and How They Shape Our Capacity to Love*. New York: Oxford University Press, 1998. If you're interested in a detailed look at the effects of upbringing on child and adult attachment, this is the one to read.

Levine, Amir, and Rachel Heller. *Attached: The New Science of Adult Attachment and How It Can Help You Find—and*

Keep—Love. New York: Jeremy P. Tarcher, 2010. Popular book with a wealth of advice and stories about how the preoccupied and dismissive can change their dating strategies and behaviors.

Johnson, Susan M. *Hold Me Tight: Seven Conversations for a Lifetime of Love*. New York: Little, Brown & Co., 2008. Another popular book with good advice on learning to be a better communicator and partner.

Anxious-Preoccupied

Shepell. Article online: "Forming Healthy Relationships with an Anxious Attachment Style."[81]

Avoidants

M.D, Martin Kantor. *Distancing: Avoidant Personality Disorder, Revised and Expanded*. Rev Exp edition. Praeger, 2003.

Therapeutic Techniques

Wallin, David J. *Attachment in Psychotherapy*. New York: Guilford Press, 2007. Highly technical book for therapists and motivated others about the therapeutic process when attachment styles are the primary issues.

Stone, Hal, and Sidra Stone. *Embracing Our Selves the Voice Dialogue Manual*. San Rafael, Calif.: New World Library, 1989.

CHAPTER THIRTY-ONE

THERAPY

So you've identified yourself as the problem with your relationships, or you have identified your attachment type as something you could work to improve to make yourself a better partner. And self-help books and talking to friends won't cut it—you want real change and are willing to work hard at it, with a professional helper. Group therapy, while valuable for getting feedback on the realism of your expectations and the actions you have taken to reach them, rarely is deep and focused enough to resolve attachment issues—the exception would be group therapy focused on one attachment type so that everyone's issues are similar, but that is hard to find.

First, in the United States and most other countries, expect to pay for individual therapy yourself. Even under the new ACA insurance plans that cover mental health treatments, an attachment issue is unlikely to be considered worthy of coverage; as in most insurance plans, you can see a psychiatrist to be prescribed a psychoactive drug, or you can see a therapist (often chosen from a limited selection, with specialists in attachment unlikely to be among them) a few times before further authorization requiring a diagnosis is required.[82] After that you will generally be on your own. And it's almost certainly true that you will find better therapists and more knowledgeable therapists if you pay their fee yourself; if your income is limited, ask the therapists you are considering if they will charge you a sliding scale fee, lower for long-term treatment on a limited income. Seeing a therapist your insurance will cover is a good way to start out, but if you find that experience unhelpful ask for referrals to more specialized therapists.

Second, there is no correct or incorrect "school" of therapy— what is important is an agile and empathetic mind willing to follow you wherever you go in a quest for understanding. One thing we do know is that Freudian theory, and the psychoanalysis that goes with it as still practiced in some places, is scientifically discredited. Freud and the other psychoanalysts have penetrated popular culture and their theories live on in metaphor and literature, though serious scholars discarded them long ago.

> Psychoanalytic concepts captivated popular culture as have no other ideas about humanity's mind and heart. But the Freudian model belongs to a prescientific era in the search to unravel the enigmas of love. The demise of such mythologies is always probable. As long as the brain remained a mystery, as long as the physical nature of the mind remained remote and inaccessible, an evidential void permitted a free flow of irrefutable statements about emotional life. As in politics, the factor determining the longevity and popularity of these notions was not their veracity but the energy and wit devoted to promoting them.

In the years when unrestrained presumptions about the mind roamed free, outlandish claims piled up like election year promises. Seizures are covert expressions of orgasmic ecstasy, one theory maintained. Children who lag in their reading and writing skills are exacting revenge on parents who expelled them from the marital bed. A migraine headache discloses sexual fantasies of defloration. All of these colorful assertions were living on time borrowed from the prevailing scientific ignorance about the brain.[83]

The great philosopher of science Karl Popper rejected Freudian thought as a scientific theory because it was not falsifiable - there was nothing it predicted that could be disproved by experiment, and it made no predictions that were actually useful in treatment. Therapists using it, and most of the other methods that have come and gone for talk therapy, are successful when they achieve an empathetic bond with the patient; therapists who are good at empathetic communication can help patients no matter what school of therapy they practice.

So what type of talk therapy is best? *It doesn't matter:*

A gathering cloud looms over the patchwork landscape of psychotherapy: the growing certainty that, despite decades of divergent rectification and elaboration, therapeutic techniques per se have nothing to do with results. The United States alone sports an inventive spectrum of psychotherapeutic sects and schools: Freudians, Jungians, Kleinians; narrative, interpersonal, transpersonal therapists; cognitive, behavioral, cognitive-behavioral practitioners; Kohutians, Rogerians, Kernbergians; aficionados of control mastery, hypnotherapy, neurolinguistic programming, eye movement desensitization—that list does not even complete the top twenty. The disparate doctrines of these proliferative, radiating divisions often reach mutually exclusive conclusions about therapeutic propriety: talk about this, not that; answer questions, or don't; sit facing the patient, next to the patient, behind the patient. Yet no approach has ever proven its method superior to any other.[84]

In Dr. Lewis' *A General Theory of Love*, he describes therapy in poetic language as a process where the therapist and the patient journey together, experiencing each other's feelings and letting the patient view his or her own interior thoughts and feelings as seen though the eyes of the therapist. The therapist serves as a secure anchor that can (metaphorically) pull the storm-tossed ship of the patient's emotional life toward a calmer shore. This only works, of course, if the patient is open to thinking about and describing his or her feelings, which is especially hard for the dismissive—the therapist may have to read between the lines and sharply question the patient's stories and rationalizations. It may take many sessions before the patient picks up the ability to dig through his or her own feelings with more insight to hold up the interesting discoveries to the light for the therapist to see.

An attuned therapist feels the lure of a patient's limbic Attractors. He doesn't just hear about an emotional life— the two of them live it. The gravitational tug of this patient's emotional world draws him away from his own, just as it should. A determined therapist does not strive to have a good relationship with his patient— it can't be done. If a patient's emotional mind would support good relationships, he or she would be out having them. Instead a therapist loosens his grip on his own world and drifts, eyes open, into whatever relationship the patient has in mind—even a connection so dark that it touches the worst in him. He has no alternative. When he stays outside the other's world, he cannot affect it; when he steps within its range, he feels the force of alien Attractors. He takes up temporary residence in another's world not just to observe but to alter, and in the end, to overthrow. Through the intimacy a limbic exchange affords, therapy becomes the ultimate inside job.[85]

In the chapter on the dismissive-avoidant type we discussed *alexithymia*, the inability to describe feelings in words, and I'll repeat that here:

The most compelling theory of how consciousness arose has between-person communication (primitive language) giving rise to internal communication, so that what we see as a stream of consciousness is actually internal dialogue, talking to yourself. Noting this, you might say that an inability to name and talk about feelings cripples your ability to be consciously aware of them. If one is very poor at doing this, one would tend to note feelings only as manifested in somatic symptoms like fast heart rate, discomfort, loss of energy, nervousness, etc.

This is why talking to someone about how you feel (or writing about it) is also training for being conscious of feelings internally. The more you talk about it to others, the more you can talk about it to yourself. Even for those not suffering from alexithymia, talking or writing about feelings can clarify understanding of them, which is one of the reasons talk therapy is effective.

Dr. Karen, in *Becoming Attached,* discusses this phenomenon of verbally describing a feeling to allow it to come under conscious control as its source is recognized:

> Main's work supports an assumption on which much of psychoanalytic treatment is based: that being able to put feelings, especially unwanted feelings, into words makes them available for review and transformation…. To have this ability means, in effect, that your internal model is still a "working" model—open, flexible, able to assimilate new information. It means not only the ability to rethink the past but to recognize that people can be different and that their behavior doesn't always mean what we think it does. The criticism of a husband or wife, for example, may feel like an intentional assault on one's identity. If you are able to attend to the feeling and put it into words—"I feel worthless and debased, convinced he wants to get rid of me, and insanely anxious and needy"—then you are in a much better position than the person who reflexively acts out such feelings by becoming depressed and over-eating or becoming uncontrollably rageful.[86]

When therapy is successful, it can not only change dysfunctional patterns of attachment behavior, but also free the patient from other habits and assumptions picked up from parents and childhood experiences and carried through life as unquestioned givens:

> The first part of emotional healing is being limbically known—having someone with a keen ear catch your melodic essence. A child with emotionally hazy parents finds trying to know himself like wandering around a museum in the dark: almost anything could exist within

its walls. He cannot ever be sure of what he senses. For adults, a precise seer's light can still split the night, illuminate treasures long thought lost, and dissolve many fearsome figures into shadows and dust. Those who succeed in revealing themselves to another find the dimness receding from their own visions of self. Like people awakening from a dream, they slough off the accumulated, ill-fitting trappings of unsuitable lives. Then the mutual fund manager may become a sculptor, or vice versa; some friendships lapse into dilapidated irrelevance as new ones deepen; the city dweller moves to the country, where he feels finally at home. As limbic clarity emerges, a life takes form.[87]

PART SEVEN

MORE ON LOVE AND ATTACHMENT THEORY

This last part delves into love and attachment at greater depth. It's not necessary knowledge for finding a good partner, but if you are interested it will fill in the picture some more.

CHAPTER THIRTY-TWO

LOVE MAKES THE WORLD GO 'ROUND

Love does really make the world go 'round. Attachment to parents, spouses, children (especially children!) and friends is the motivating force for most achievement beyond simple material survival, and our roles as protectors and defenders of loved ones are built into us by millennia of evolution. Our ancestors all succeeded at protecting their families from famine and death, or we would never have been born; and the limbic spurs to act for others are so powerful they even extend to strangers. It is not an unusual story for a passerby to endanger him or herself to rescue a perfect stranger in distress. The dead-end job, the boring commute, the grind of daily life, are endured for those moments when our family and friends acknowledge us. We want to be esteemed, and we want to be loved, and to love.

But most of us are working in the dark, with little but the fairy tale of romance and similar child's stories to guide us. The toll on the productivity of the world due to bad relationships, broken families, neglected children, and loneliness is enormous. So researchers asking questions about attachment and developmental neuroscience are working on some of the most important and neglected problems of our technical age: the life guidelines handed down to us from our hunter-gatherer and agricultural village heritage have failed to keep up, when children text their friends on other continents and adults are run ragged by lives of extreme multitasking and overcommitment. This is why these studies are so important—knowing more gives us the ability to guide and control our lives for greater fulfillment.

> The investigation of these queries is not just an intellectual excursion: people must have the answers to make sense of their lives. We see the need for this knowledge every day, and we see the bitter consequences of its lack. People who do not intuit or respect the laws of acceleration and momentum break bones; those who do not grasp the principles of love waste their lives and break their hearts. The evidence of that pain surrounds us, in the form of failed marriages, hurtful relationships, neglected children, unfulfilled ambitions, and thwarted dreams. And in numbers, these injuries combine to damage our society, where emotional suffering and its ramifications are commonplace. The roots of that suffering are often unseen and passed over, while proposed remedies cannot succeed, because they contradict emotional laws that our culture does not yet recognize.[88]

CHAPTER THIRTY-THREE

FEELINGS: WHAT GOOD ARE THEY?

> We say, "I will," and "I will not," and imagine ourselves
> (though we obey the orders of some prosaic person every
> day) our own masters, when the truth is that our masters
> are sleeping. One wakes within us, and we are ridden like
> beasts, though the rider is but some hitherto unguessed
> part of ourselves.   Gene Wolfe

As discussed in *Chapter One: The Triune Brain,* the limbic
system takes situational and sensory input and generates
emotions and defensive imperatives that go beyond
instinctive; for example, a mammal may instinctively shy
from a snake, but humans may also have developed a higher-
level emotion of disgust, fear, and avoidance based on the
instinctive response and additive experience, or the expressed
emotions of others (as you grow up seeing your parents react
to threats, you absorb an echo of their fear.) These high-level
emotions can be modified by experience, so that with
training snake-handlers are able to calmly engage with their
snakes. But since these fear responses are embedded below
the conscious, verbal level, one cannot simply decide to
overrule them to handle snakes—a longer process of
retraining is required.

The author personally experienced the full force of this limbic emotional processing in his days of running through Stanley Park (a dark fir and cedar forest) in Vancouver. One spring, the population of young owls boomed—so many were born that their parents were unable to properly train and supervise them all. As a result, the young owls trying out their hunting skills tried to attack and pick up the heads of dozens of human runners, sending some to the emergency room—untrained, they instinctively saw the bobbing heads of the runners as running small animal prey. I was attacked three times, the final time turning to confront and wave away the owl flapping in front of my face. What came as a revelation to me was the irrational and completely uncontrollable fear that I felt for months afterward, set off by certain isolated and dark parts of the forest trails that were subconsciously seen as matching the pattern of places where I had been attacked. Thus our feelings are triggered by pattern-matching of the current situation with similar past situations, and we may be "ridden like beasts" by these emotions.

Our attachment feelings are similarly inchoate and uncontrollable. When they are positive they can spur the best of human striving; when they are negative, conflict and violence can result. Our overlying verbal and conscious processing may be able to transmute and partially contain these feelings, but sometimes will be unable to keep up with rationalizing them:

> The verbal rendition of emotional material thus demands a difficult transmutation. And so people must strain to force a strong feeling into the straitjacket of verbal

expression. Often, as emotionality rises, so do sputtering, gesticulation, and mute frustration. Poetry, a bridge between the neocortical and limbic brains, is simultaneously improbable and powerful. Frost wrote that a poem "begins as a lump in the throat, a sense of wrong, a homesickness, a love sickness. It is never a thought to begin with."[89]

Emotions also play a key role in decisionmaking. In computer science and machine learning (a good example being a chess playing program), the algorithm for making a decision starts by deciding what choices are available, evaluating a choice by following each possible decision's likely consequences and the decisions that may follow from that, etc., all the way down the line; all possibilities are looked at and a decision chosen. This branching of alternatives is the *decision tree*, which tries to predict the future after any proposed action and pick the most advantageous choice. Since the number of possible outcomes that has to be evaluated grows rapidly as you look further down the tree into the future, *treepruning*[90] (heuristics that stop the evaluation when branches of the tree appear unpromising) is required to keep the decision space manageable. And emotions are a key part of the human heuristic for making decisions. Like generalizations about the desirability of recognized patterns in chess, a decisionmaker's feelings are based on the generalized outcomes of similar situations previously experienced and *felt,* and are used to simply discard without further thought many of the possible choices because they don't "feel right."

It is widely assumed that emotion and rationality are

somehow opposed to each other, and that rational decisions are better than emotional ones. In fact, emotion and reason work closely together, as has been demonstrated by Antonio Damasio....

Dr Damasio, who now works at the University of Southern California, is both a clinician and a researcher.... He has a patient called Elliot (in neuroscience, patients are often referred to by single names or initials to preserve their privacy) whose frontal lobe was damaged by a brain tumour. When the tumour was removed by surgeons, the damaged tissue was taken out too.

Like [a famous historical case, Gage], Elliot was a responsible individual with a good job (and in his case a family, too) before he suffered his brain damage. The outcome was somewhat different in that Elliot did not become a foul-mouthed wastrel; rather, he became obsessed with detail and stopped being able to make sensible decisions. The overall result was similar, though. He lost his job and his wife and ended up an outcast.

At first, Dr Damasio thought that Elliot's tumour had damaged his reason (both lesion studies and fMRI have shown that the frontal cortex is also the seat of the brain's reasoning powers). Tests, however, showed that what had gone instead were his emotions. Elliot no longer felt anything, and although he could summarise the choices available in a given situation as well as anyone else, without his emotions to guide him he could not actually make a choice. And, as probably happened with Gage, that loss of emotion also changed his self.

The survival value of things like fear, disgust and joy is

obvious: run away from it; don't eat it; do more of it. But the idea that emotions shape all activity in adaptive ways is quite a subtle one. Rationality has its place. In the end, though, as fans of "Star Trek" will remember, it is Captain Kirk, the emotion-ridden human, not Mr Spock, the emotionless Vulcan, who has the nous to run the spaceship.[91]

This is why those who have less direct access to their library of emotional memories are also likely to flounder when required to make a decision; this is notably true of some of the alexithymic dismissive. You can be brilliant and very good at evaluating possibilities, but without the ability to *stop* evaluating and act on feeling, much time will be wasted. This is another reason for the high incidence of psychopathic traits among upper level corporate managers; they are still highly motivated by a desire to win, but they are less afraid of the negative feelings that the thousands under them and their peers at competitors might have about their decisions, and so arrive at them more quickly—and in many business conflicts, like wartime battlefields, a delayed decision can be fatal.

If you could hear the feelings of those around you, your community would be a buzz of noisy positive and negative feelings, many of them frightening, and most of them hidden from others. Social life is not much advanced from the hominid bands we evolved from, and while we have a sophisticated overlay of words and symbols, the secret we keep from ourselves is how much our "primitive" feelings and attachment lessons learned in the first two years of life control our behavior. Learning to recognize this and support those around us by providing them with the most honest possible communication—and our children with the most responsive but non-intrusive support—would go a long way toward making the world a better and happier place.

> Our society underplays the importance of emotions. Having allied itself with the neocortical brain, our culture promotes analysis over intuition, logic above feeling. Cognition can yield riches, and human intellect has made our lives easier in ways that range from indoor plumbing to the Internet. But even as it reaps the benefits of reason, modern America plows emotions under—a costly practice that obstructs happiness and misleads people about the nature and significance of their lives.

> That deliberate imbalance is more damaging than one might suppose. Beyond the variegated sensations and the helpful motivations, science has discovered emotionality's deeper purpose: the timeworn mechanisms of emotion allow two human beings to receive the contents of each other's minds. Emotion is the messenger of love; it is the vehicle that carries every signal from one brimming heart to another. For human beings, feeling deeply is synonymous with being alive.[92]

Chapter Thirty-Four

Limbic Resonance

Limbic resonance[93] is a term first used in *A General Theory of Love;* it is the theory that the limbic systems of individuals are connected, and regulated by interactions between them ranging from touch and smell to conversations and facial expressions. Resonance means feelings are contagious: sensing distress, we are distressed; and sensing happiness, we are likely to be happier.

> The limbic brain is another delicate physical apparatus that specializes in detecting and analyzing just one part of the physical world—the internal state of other mammals. Emotionality is the social sense organ of limbic creatures. While vision lets us experience the reflected wavelengths of electromagnetic radiation, and hearing gives information about the pressure waves in the surrounding air, emotionality enables a mammal to sense the inner states and the motives of the mammals around him. [94]

Higher mammals all have this ability within their own species, and our limbic systems have features in common with them to such an extent that domesticated animals with a long history of living with humans can sense our feelings:

But most emotions require no thinking at all. For years, patients have told us stories about pets coming to their side and comforting them when they were distraught. Our medical training (often more hindrance than help in matters of the heart) led us to greet this allegation with a skeptical eye. How could a dog or a cat, with its diminutive brain, apprehend a phenomenon as complex as human emotion? One might as well expect an armadillo to master algebra. But cats and dogs are mammals—neocortically primitive and limbically mature. The limbic ancestry they share with humans should allow them to read and respond to certain emotional states of their owners. So when a person says he has a cat that can tell when he's had a bad day and hides under the bed, or a dog that detects sorrow and comes to console him, we no longer think he is being extravagantly anthropomorphic. The reciprocal process is dead easy: a perceptive human can tell if a dog is fatigued, contented, fearful, guilty, playful, hostile, or excited.

Not so with an animal that predates the limbic brain—try reading the inner state of a turtle, a goldfish, or an iguana. Animals with a common phylogenetic history share trait similarities: just as there are wide resemblances in the bony structure of the wrist or ankle among mammals, so too are there underlying commonalities in emotional perception and expression. Variants of the same emotional language exist throughout the mammalian family, some incomprehensible to us and others relatively close and accessible to our interpretative instrument, the limbic brain.[95]

A human infant is helpless in its first year of life compared to the young of most animals. Born with a brain as large as could be fit through the birth canal, its brain is still small and will grow rapidly in the first few years of life. Its brain is also disorganized, and requires years of responsive communication from others to properly organize the capacity to communicate and feel necessary for its adult social existence. But the one ability it does have almost from birth is to get its needs satisfied by intuiting the emotions of its caregivers:

> But an infant doesn't check up on his mother's face only when ambiguity threatens—babies continuously monitor their mothers' expressions. If a mother freezes her face, her baby becomes upset and begins to cry in short order. How much expressiveness do babies demand? Imagine a double video camera setup, in which mother and baby can see each other, but not face-to-face; each sees the other in their respective monitors. In real time, mother and infant look at each other, smile and laugh, and both are perfectly happy. If the baby sees a videotape of his mother's face instead of the real-time display, he quickly becomes distraught. It isn't just his mother's beaming countenance but her synchrony that he requires— their mutually responsive interaction. Restore his mother's face in real time to his TV monitor, and his contentment returns. Introduce a delay into the video circuit, and the baby will again become distressed.

An infant can detect minute temporal changes in emotional responsiveness. This level of sophistication is coming from an organism that won't be able to stand up on his own for another six months. Why should a creature with relatively few skills be so monomaniacally focused on tiny muscular contractions visible beneath the skin of another creature's body? The answer lies in the evolutionary history of the limbic brain. Animals have highly developed neural systems for processing specific informational needs. The sonar system of bats serves them admirably in chasing small bugs in a pitch-black night; within the cacophony of their high-pitched echoes, they can see a world we are blind to. The intricate cellular structure of certain eels allows the precise mapping of perturbations in nearby electric fields; the eel recognizes other fish, including its prey, by the pattern of electricity their muscles cast off.[96]

What happens when a human grows up with normal or even brilliant intellectual capabilities, but limited or damaged social abilities? When they are unable to "listen" to the hearts of others through limbic resonance?

The Viennese pediatrician Hans Asperger first described this affliction in the 1940s; it is now known as Asperger's syndrome. Children with Asperger's can be intellectually bright or brilliant, but they are emotionally clumsy, tone-deaf to social subtleties in others, and sometimes to their own emotions. When we asked a young woman with Asperger's what made her unhappy, she was quick to correct us: "I know that the words happy and unhappy signify something to other people, and I have heard others use them, but I do not know what they mean," she told us. "As far as I know, I have had no experience of either. I have no basis on which to answer your question."[97]

Chapter Thirty-Five

Development of Attachment Theory

There are several scholarly books on the development of adult attachment theory as an outgrowth of studies in child development. Lewis, Amini, and Lannon's *A General Theory of Love*[98] has an excellent introduction to the topic, and Karen's *Becoming Attached: First Relationships and How They Shape Our Capacity to Love*[99] goes into greater detail.

The key insight came from observations of mother and child interactions, and how they seemed to affect the children's social engagement with both their mothers and others:

> More than twenty years ago, developmental psychologist Mary Ainsworth investigated mothers and their newborn infants and found that the kind of mother a baby has predicts his emotional traits in later life. She first watched how mothers looked after babies and divided caretaking styles into three categories. A year later, Ainsworth then tested the children's emotionality by observing their response to brief separations. A mother who had been consistently attentive, responsive, and tender to her infant raised a secure child, who used his mother as a safe haven from which to explore the world. He was upset and fussy when she left him and reassured and joyful when she came

back. A cold, resentful, rigid mother produced an insecure-avoidant child, who displayed indifference to his mother's departures and often pointedly ignored her on her return, turning his back or crawling away to a suddenly fascinating toy in the corner. The baby of a mother distracted or erratic in her attentions became an insecure-ambivalent toddler, clutching at his mother when they were together, dissolving into wails and shrieks when the two were separated, and remaining inconsolable after their reunion.

As the children matured, mothers' parenting aptitude predicted more and more budding personality traits. Babies of responsive mothers developed into grade-schoolers who were happy, socially competent, resilient, persistent, likable, and empathic with others. They had more friends, were relaxed about intimacy, solved problems on their own when they could, and sought help when they needed it. Infants reared by the cold mothers grew up to be distant, difficult-to-reach kids who were hostile to authority, shunned togetherness, and and seemed to take pleasure in provoking and upsetting other children. The offspring of the unpredictable mothers metamorphosed into children who were socially inept, timid, hypersensitive, and lacking in confidence. Hungry for attention and easily frustrated, they frequently asked for assistance with simple tasks that should have been within their competence.[100]

Another insight from the studies of child development is suggestive of the ideal adult partner or close friend interaction:

Ainsworth found no simple correlation between the

length of time a mother spent attending to her child and his ultimate emotional health. The securely attached children were not necessarily the infants who were taken up into their mothers' arms most frequently or held the longest. Ainsworth observed instead that secure attachment resulted when a child was hugged when he wanted to be hugged and put down when he wanted to be put down. When he was hungry, his mother knew it and fed him; when he began to tire, his mother felt it and eased his transition into sleep by tucking him into his bassinet. Wherever a mother sensed her baby's inarticulate desires and acted on them, not only was their mutual enjoyment greatest, but the outcome was, years later, a secure child.[101]

It is the appropriateness of the response provided by the other based on the correct intuition of need that matters.

General Books on Attachment

Lewis, Thomas, Fari Amini, and Richard Lannon. *A General Theory of Love*. New York: Vintage Books, 2001. This book is a groundbreaking synthesis of recent scientific work in the study of attachment. Assuming you have a high school science background, it emotionally moving and accessible, and brings together topics of neuroscience and psychology with an entertaining literary sensibility. Should be required reading in college psychology courses.

Karen, Robert. *Becoming Attached: First Relationships and How They Shape Our Capacity to Love*. New York: Oxford University Press, 1998. If you're interested in a detailed look at the effects of upbringing on child and adult attachment, this is the one to read.

Levine, Amir, and Rachel Heller. *Attached: The New Science of Adult Attachment and How It Can Help You Find—and Keep—Love*. New York: Jeremy P. Tarcher, 2010. Popular book with a wealth of advice and stories about how the anxious and dismissive can change their dating strategies and behaviors.

Johnson, Susan M. *Hold Me Tight: Seven Conversations for a Lifetime of Love*. New York: Little, Brown & Co., 2008. Another popular book with good advice on learning to be a better communicator and partner.

Subpersonalities

Rowan, John. *Subpersonalities: The People Inside Us*. Routledge, 2013. Our stream of consciousness includes messages to direct our own actions—but what voice has the floor? It can be useful to look at conscious thought as an agora where internal subpersonalities struggle to be heard and control our actions. This can be especially helpful when a subpersonality that represents the overprotective or oppressive parental voice is identifiable and is distorting the thinking of the child in adulthood.

Therapeutic Techniques

Wallin, David J. *Attachment in Psychotherapy*. New York: Guilford Press, 2007. Highly technical book for therapists and motivated others about the therapeutic process when attachment styles are the primary issues.

Stone, Hal, and Sidra Stone. *Embracing Our Selves: the Voice Dialogue Manual*. San Rafael, Calif.: New World Library, 1989.

Acknowledgements

Thanks to those authors who have inspired and educated me on this science of the heart, notably Drs. Lewis, Amini, and Lannon, who wrote the seminal synthesis, *A General Theory of Love*. Thanks also to early readers and critics: Stewart Kramer at Stanford, Eric Jannke, Alex Roederer, Lou Ceci, and David O on Planet O. And thanks to Drs. Cindy Hazan and Phillip Shaver, who could be called the founders of Adult Attachment Theory, for doing their pioneering work and commenting supportively in correspondence.

And most of all, I thank my husband and partner for the hours of proofreading, contributions, and inspiration. The ideas and opinions in this book were formed by hours of discussion, email, and blog postings, so it is really a collaborative work.

[Cover art: Courtship. Tondo of an Ancient Greek Attic red-figure kylix, ca. 480 BC, from Vulci. Louvre Museum, Paris. Department of Greek, Etruscan and Roman Antiquities, 1st floor, room 43, case 24. Signed by Hieron as potter and Macron as painter.]

Online Resources

For up-to-date news on relationship topics and the author's work, please go to my web site at **jebkinnison.com**, and if you want to be regularly notified of updates, sign up for my mailing list there. Since online resources change frequently, I'll have a groomed list of better web sites there for further exploration.

If you'd like to email me directly with questions, errata, or comments, I'm at **jebkinnison@gmail.com**.

About the Author

I grew up in the Midwest, child of a schizophrenic father and a hardworking single mother. At 12, I was deemed brilliant but uncontrollable, and I was sent to a private psychiatric hospital, where I was grilled about my sexual fantasies (which, not surprisingly, made me acutely uncomfortable). But this experience had me spending a lot of time with psychologists and psychiatric residents, which got me interested in the topic.

I studied computer and cognitive science at MIT, and wrote programs modeling the behavior of simulated stock traders and the population dynamics of economic agents. Later I did supercomputer work at a think tank that developed parts of the early Internet (where the engineer who decided on '@' as the separator for email addresses worked down the hall.) Since then I have had several careers—real estate, financial advising, and counselling. I retired at 47 to write and explain how things *really* work.

In attachment terms, in high school I was behind in social development and had to learn about people to catch up. So I started my 20s mildly anxious-preoccupied, had two lengthy but imperfect relationships, and finally matured into a more secure type—and when I was around 40, met my most excellent partner.

Notes

[1] See the graph in Chapter "The Search" showing how the proportion of secure types declines in the dating pool with age.

[2] Note that much recent work has shown that some birds and reptiles have advanced capabilities in memory, object recognition, and even self-awareness, so it appears that their evolutionary development on a parallel path to mammals has given them some "higher" capabilities.

[3] Personal email from Dr. Philip Shaver: "There are ten times as many neurons in the brain as there are people on earth, and each neuron has, on average, way more connections with other neurons than most humans do with other humans. So the brain is pretty complex. Whenever I hear a neuroscientist say s/he is trying to create a theory of the brain, I think about the impossibility of a 'theory' of New York City, where I lived for 10 years. Every day, zillions of flowers are delivered to the city and distributed to hundreds of local florists; hundreds of police officers cruise around the city in organized patterns; hospitals admit and treat thousands of patients; Broadway shows are performed every evening; a mayor's office (like "executive functions" in the brain) try to keep everything reasonably organized; etc., etc. There is no theory of New York City that makes sense of all this. And there is no theory of the brain/mind either. So everyone has to piece together a reasonable explanation of particular phenomena. As soon as someone tries to do this, someone else shows that the story isn't that simple. (The amygdala, for example, which is often presented as the seat of emotion, or at least of fear, has numerous parts with different functions; the same goes for the hypothalamus, the cingulate, and the nucleus accumbens. It will be a long time before it's all figured out.)"

[4] Mikulincer, M., Shaver, P.R., & Pereg, D. (2003). Attachment theory and affect regulation: The dynamics, development, and cognitive consequences of attachment-related strategies. *Motivation and Emotion*, 27, 77–102.

[5] From http://en.wikipedia.org/wiki/Attachment_in_adults

[6] Bretherton I (1992). "The Origins of Attachment Theory: John Bowlby and Mary Ainsworth". *Developmental Psychology* **28** (5): 759.

[7] Hazan, Cindy, and Shaver, Philip (1987). "Romantic Love Conceptualized as an Attachment Process". Journal of Personality and Social Psychology 52 (3):511-524. http://www2.psych.ubc.ca/~schaller/Psyc591Readings/HazanShaver1987.pdf

[8] http://internal.psychology.illinois.edu/~rcfraley/
R. Chris Fraley, University of Illinois at Urbana-Champaign, Department of Psychology, 603 East Daniel Street, Champaign, IL 61820

[9] Karen, Robert. *Becoming Attached: First Relationships and How They Shape Our Capacity to Love*. New York: Oxford University Press, 1998.
p. 388

[10] Baumeister; Tierney (2011). *Willpower: the Greatest Human Strength*. p. 192.

[11] Maslow's original conception was oversimplified, and he later promoted a more nuanced view.

[12] Goldman, Daniel. "Emotional Intelligence," 1995 Bantam

[13] Karen, p. 364

[14] Karen, p. 372

[15] Karen, p. 382

[16] Levine and Heller, p. 136

[17] Karen, p. 366

[18] Karen, p. 372

[19] Karen, p. 375

[20] Karen, p. 383

[21] Karen, p. 385

[22] Karen, p. 399

[23] Karen, p. 387

[24] Peele, Stanton, and Archie Brodsky. *Love and Addiction*. New York: Penguin Group, 1991.

[25] Shepell, "Forming Healthy Relationships with an Anxious Attachment Style." *Workhealthlife Blog*. Accessed February 4, 2014. http://blog.workhealthlife.com/2012/10/forming-healthy-relationships-with-an-anxious-attachment-style/.

[26] Levine, Amir, and Rachel Heller. *Attached: The New Science of Adult Attachment and How It Can Help You Find—and Keep—Love*. New York: Jeremy P. Tarcher, 2010.

[27] Karen, p. 365

[28] Karen, p. 383

[29] Karen, p. 384

[30] Karen, p. 399

[31] Karen, p. 387

[32] Levine and Heller, p. 117

[33] http://en.wikipedia.org/wiki/Alexithymia

[34] Kantor, Martin. *Distancing: Avoidant Personality Disorder, Revised and Expanded*. Rev Exp edition. Praeger, 2003.

[35] "Q&A: Can I Change Someone with an Avoidant Attachment Style? | YourTango." Accessed February 4, 2014. http://www.yourtango.com/201167909/qa-can-i-change-someone-avoidant-attachment-style.

[36] "Approach-Avoidance Conflict." *Wikipedia, the Free Encyclopedia*, January 4, 2014. http://en.wikipedia.org/w/index.php?title=Approach-avoidance_conflict&oldid=589161815.

[37] Karen, p. 373

[38] Miller, Alice. *The Drama of the Gifted Child: The Search for the True Self, Revised Edition*. Basic Books, 1996.
The author lost me quickly in the forward by implying that all mental illness comes from childhood abuse; not true, since most truly crazy people have treatable defects in brain chemistry and were nurtured just fine. Then there's the suggestion that a friend died of cancer because of his mishandling of feelings about his parents.

She has a hammer (abuse and her pet therapy) and everything looks like a nail. Her oblique references to "perversions" and suggestion that those are defense mechanisms, too, is nonsense. The book is full of her emotional prejudices and ignores the research done in this exact area of failed early nurturing by narcissistic or negligent mothers. She further muddies issues by failing to distinguish between attachment disorders created by narcissistic nurturers—who make their love conditional on supporting the needs of the caregiver—and physical or sexual abuse, which should be considered separately.

[39] Stone, Hal, and Sidra Stone. *Embracing Your Inner Critic: Turning Self-Criticism into a Creative Asset.* [San Francisco]: HarperSanFrancisco, 1993.

[40] Rowan, John. *Subpersonalities: The People Inside Us.* Routledge, 2013.

[41] Fallon, James H. *The Psychopath inside: A Neuroscientist's Personal Journey into the Dark Side of the Brain.* New York: Current, 2013.

[42] Karen, p. 390

[43] Karen, p. 390

[44] Kernberg, O.F. (1970). "Factors in the psychoanalytic treatment of narcissistic personalities." Journal of the American Psychoanalytic Association, 18:51–85

[45] Jordan, C. H.; Spencer, S. J.; Zanna, M. P., Hoshino-Browne, E.; Correll, J. (2003). "Secure and defensive high self-esteem". *Journal of Personality and Social Psychology* 85 (5): 969–978. "A person can have a high self-esteem and hold it confidently where they do not need reassurance from others to maintain their positive self view, whereas others with defensive, high self-esteem may still report positive self-evaluations on the Rosenberg Scale, as all high self-esteem individuals do; however, their positive self-views are fragile and vulnerable to criticism. Defensive high self-esteem individuals internalize subconscious self-doubts and insecurities causing them to react very negatively to any criticism they may receive. There is a need for constant positive feedback from others for these individuals to maintain their feelings of self-worth. The necessity of repeated praise can be associated with boastful, arrogant behavior or sometimes even aggressive and hostile

feelings toward anyone who questions the individual's self-worth, an example of threatened egotism." http://en.wikipedia.org/wiki/Self-esteem

[46] http://well.blogs.nytimes.com/2013/09/16/everyday-sadists-among-us/

[47] Oxford Textbook of Psychopathology. The DSM is periodically revised, and this category is not one of the best defined ones. More commonly sadism is a trait manifested with other dysfunctional traits.

[48] http://samvak.tripod.com/personalitydisorders31.html

[49] James, E. L. *Fifty Shades of Grey*. New York: Vintage Books, 2012.

[50] http://www.manipulative-people.com/demeaning-as-a-lifestyle-the-sadistic-aggressive/

[51] http://www.businessinsider.com/how-do-you-know-if-youre-a-psychopath-2013-2?op=1

[52] Fallon, James H. *The Psychopath inside: A Neuroscientist's Personal Journey into the Dark Side of the Brain*. New York: Current, 2013.

[53] Pinkofsky, H B. "Mnemonics for DSM-IV Personality Disorders." Psychiatric Services (Washington, D.C.) 48, no. 9 (September 1997): 1197–1198.

[54] Karen, p. 392

[55] Karen, p. 381

[56] Karen, p. 382

[57] Parker-pope, Tara. "Is Marriage Good for Your Health?" *The New York Times*, April 14, 2010, sec. Magazine. http://www.nytimes.com/2010/04/18/magazine/18marriage-t.html.

[58] Oppenheimer, Mark. "Dan Savage on the Virtues of Infidelity." *The New York Times*, June 30, 2011, sec. Magazine. http://www.nytimes.com/2011/07/03/magazine/infidelity-will-keep-us-together.html.

[59] Personal communication.

[60] http://en.wikipedia.org/wiki/Dorothy_Tennov

[61] Tennov, Dorothy (1999). *Love and Limerence: The Experience*

of Being in Love. Scarborough House. ISBN 978-0-8128-6286-7.

[62] http://en.wikipedia.org/wiki/Limerence

[63] A fascinating operetta by Stephen Sondheim about obsessive limerence and its persuasive power : Lapine, James. *Stephen Sondheim's Passion*. Image Entertainment, 2003.

[64] Lewis, p 206

[65] Roxy Music's *Love Is The Drug*:   https://www.youtube.com/watch?v=0n3OepDn5GU&feature=kp

[66] Peele, Stanton, and Archie Brodsky. *Love and Addiction*. New York: Penguin Group, 1991.

[67] Lewis, p 207

[68] http://en.wikipedia.org/wiki/The_seven-year_itch

[69] Lewis, p 101

[70] Karen, p. 404

[71] Levine, Amir; Heller, Rachel (2010-12-30). Attached: The New Science of Adult Attachment and How It Can Help You Find—and Keep—Love. p/ 91, Penguin Group US

[72] Levine and Heller, p. 96

[73] Karen, p. 372

[74] This graph is based on data from a simplified simulation model run by the author based on reported duration of relationships by attachment type combinations and initial populations. Suggestive, but the initial parameters are based on limited studies and the simulation ignores such factors as longer relationships tending to break down less frequently. More longitudinal studies are needed.

[75] Levine, Amir, and Rachel Heller. *Attached: The New Science of Adult Attachment and How It Can Help You Find—and Keep—Love*. New York: Jeremy P. Tarcher, 2010.

[76] Grossman, Lev. *The Magicians: A Novel*. New York: Plume, 2010.

[77] Karen, p. 406

[78] Karen, p. 396

[79] Karen, p. 397

[80] Lewis, p 177

[81] Shepell. "Forming Healthy Relationships with an Anxious Attachment Style." *Workhealthlife Blog*. Accessed February 4, 2014. http://blog.workhealthlife.com/2012/10/forming-healthy-relationships-with-an-anxious-attachment-style/.

[82] "An Update on How the U.S. Affordable Care Act Impacts Mental Health Care - World of Psychology." *Psych Central.com*. Accessed February 27, 2014. http://psychcentral.com/blog/archives/2013/11/01/an-update-on-how-the-u-s-affordable-care-act-impacts-mental-health-care/.

[83] Lewis, p. 8

[84] Lewis. p 186

[85] Lewis, p 278

[86] Karen, p. 370

[87] Lewis, p 170

[88] Lewis, p. 13

[89] Lewis, p. 34

[90] http://en.wikipedia.org/wiki/Pruning_(decision_trees)

[91] http://www.economist.com/node/8407277 Dec. 19, 2006

[92] Lewis, p. 37

[93] http://en.wikipedia.org/wiki/Limbic_resonance

[94] Lewis, p. 42

[95] Lewis, p. 42

[96] Lewis, p. 42

[97] Lewis, p. 56

[98] Lewis, Thomas, Fari Amini, and Richard Lannon. *A General Theory of Love*. New York: Vintage Books, 2001.

[99] Karen, Robert. *Becoming Attached: First Relationships and How They Shape Our Capacity to Love*. New York: Oxford University Press, 1998.

[100] Lewis, p. 73

[101] Lewis, p. 75

97890677R00124

Made in the USA
San Bernardino, CA
26 November 2018